W9-CLI-717

"If you're not a Calvinist, this book is for you; and if you are a Calvinist, this book is for you. Down to earth, often funny, and with a keen knack for illustration, Medders makes plain what biblical Calvinism—humble Calvinism—looks like in everyday life."

DONALD S. WHITNEY, Author, *Praying the Bible*

"Laugh-out-loud Reformed theology. This is a book for our sectarian times: a delightful cornucopia of sprightly prose, fresh insights, and heartfelt self-examination. At times I found myself guffawing through the funny-bone pain of his all-too-accurate descriptions of the company of the Reformed. "

KEVIN J. VANHOOZER, Research Professor of Systematic Theology, Trinity Evangelical Divinity School

"Jeff speaks straight to the elephant in the echo chamber, showing himself to be the chief of prideful Calvinists and charting his subsequent journey toward humble Calvinism. Beautiful writing with rich theology."

LORE FERGUSON WILBERT, Author, *Handle With Care*

"Calvinists should be humble and happy. It's sadly not always the case, and 'Young, Restless and Reformed' has too often become 'Proud, Aggressive and Tiresome.' Medders has done us all—and me in particular—a very great service in providing some necessary correction and some great encouragement."

ADRIAN REYNOLDS, Associate National Director, FIEC UK

"Reformed culture seems to be known for its harshness and lack of grace. Yet Reformed soteriology should create a joyful heart and a deep, glad humility that overflows into compassionate evangelism and graciousness to all. I hope Jeff's book will be used by God to renew a spirit of gentleness and humility among us, and will encourage those who have rejected these beautiful beliefs to consider them anew."

MATT CHANDLER, Lead Pastor, The Village Church, Dallas; President, Acts 29; Author, *Take Heart*

"Too often, we allow our personal theological perspectives to divide us when God calls for unity. I'm thankful for this call for empathy, understanding, and humility. Regardless of whether your theology is Reformed or not, I hope you'll process the principles from this book and put them into action."

CALEB KALTENBACH, Author, *Messy Grace*

"I knew the ins and outs of Calvinism well before I understood the ins and outs of God's grace, which is an insane thing to write—but also why Jeff's book is so valuable. I likely would have been too arrogant to appreciate it then, but, looking back, it is exactly the message I desperately needed as a young Reformed guy. I'm so grateful this book is available now, and I pray it will save some other cocksure Calvinist from themselves."

BARNABAS PIPER, Podcaster; Author, *The Pastor's Kid*

"Read this if you are a Calvinist. Read it if you don't understand Calvinism. Read it if you dislike Calvinism! I am certain you'll be encouraged, and you might even be pleasantly surprised. Both timely and helpful, from the first page to the last this refreshing book encouraged me to delight in Jesus, the author and finisher of our faith."

STEVE TIMMIS, CEO, Acts 29; Author, *Total Church*

"A great book on how to be robustly Reformed and savor the doctrines of grace without being a jerk about it. I wish I had read this book when I was in seminary. It is about how theological knowledge and Christ-like love go together; and if they don't, then you're doing it wrong."

MICHAEL F. BIRD, Lecturer in Theology, Ridley College, Melbourne, Australia

"Maybe in another generation the term 'humble Calvinism' won't seem like such an oxymoron. If so, this encouraging and challenging book will have been used by God to help us live up to what we believe."

COLLIN HANSEN, Editorial Director, The Gospel Coalition; Author, *Young, Restless, and Reformed*

"I am a truer Calvinist and a happier Christian having read this book. Like a physician, Jeff carefully diagnosed pride in areas that I did not know existed and then prescribed the only cure—the glorious gospel of grace."

MATT BOSWELL, Hymnwriter; Pastor, The Trails Church, Celina, Texas

"This wonderful book serves as a wake-up call for that part of us that tends to be more doctrinaire than doctrinal, with a knowledge that puffs up instead of a love that builds up. An excellent—not to mention refreshing—way forward."

SCOTT SAULS, Senior Pastor, Christ Presbyterian Church, Nashville; Author, *Befriend*

"Experience isn't the best teacher. Someone else's experience is. You learn the same lesson without paying the same price. I'm grateful for Jeff's book for this reason. He charts a course through the landmines of Calvinism with the shrewdness (and sympathy) of someone who's recklessly walked the path and lost a few limbs in the process, leading us to a deep love and humility."

JOHN ONWUCHEKWA, Pastor, Cornerstone Church, Atlanta

J. A. MEDDERS

FOREWORD BY
RAY ORTLUND

HUMBLE

CALVINISM

AND IF I KNOW THE

5
POINTS

BUT HAVE NOT LOVE...

AFTERWORD BY
C. H. SPURGEON

thegoodbook
COMPANY

Humble Calvinism
© 2019 J. A. Medders

Published by:
The Good Book Company

thegoodbook.com | www.thegoodbook.co.uk
thegoodbook.com.au | thegoodbook.co.nz | thegoodbook.co.in

Published in association with Don Gates of The Gates Group,
www.the-gates-group.com

A CIP catalogue record for this book is available from the British Library.

ISBN: 9781784983727 | Printed in the UK

Design by André Parker

CONTENTS

To my brothers and sisters in Acts 29 churches
all around the world.

May we be humble and happy Calvinists.

FOREWORD
BY RAY ORTLUND

Calvinism is exciting. As a way of gaining new insights into the Bible, as a God-centered way of seeing all of reality, Calvinism is exciting. The God of Calvin, Owen, Edwards, Spurgeon, Machen, Lloyd-Jones, Schaeffer and many others, the God of the Heidelberg Catechism, the Westminster Confession of Faith, and the 1689 Baptist Confession—the glorious God envisioned by these thinkers and displayed through these documents is compelling to more and more Christians today. "Reformed" theology has made a big comeback. It's a good time to be a Calvinist.

The sad part is, we corrupt everything we touch. That too is a teaching of Calvinism, and we sure are proving it. Let's all admit the complication we too often introduce. It works like this. The very fact that Calvinism is intellectually satisfying, and even thrilling, can make us feel superior to other Christians who don't "get it" yet. Then we Calvinists become oblivious to how annoying we are in attempting to spread our beliefs to others who are unconvinced. Glorious theology, conveyed through an immature personality, ends up seeming inglorious and even distasteful.

A humble Arminian can be a good Christian. But a proud Calvinist cannot be a good Christian or a good Calvinist. One of the clearest messages from one end of the Bible to the other is summed up like this: "God opposes the proud but gives grace to the humble" (James 4 v 6). Any theology that is technically accurate but personally self-exalting does harm not only to people but also to that very theology. Above all, in relishing the fine points of theological debate we can lose sight of Jesus himself, without our even realizing it. Then we Calvinists leave behind us a trail of destruction in our churches and families and friendships. In this respect, we Calvinists might be the ones who don't "get it" yet.

But the fault is not in Reformed theology itself. That theology, so true to the Bible and honoring to the Lord, is in fact a wonderfully humbling power. It puts us down on our faces before the Lord, where we are happy, winsome, and fruitful. And that is how *Humble Calvinism* by Pastor Jeff Medders can help us all.

This book needed to be written, to guide us into the very humility that Calvinism should create. If God is big and we are small, if God's power jump-starts us without our help, if the only contribution we make to our salvation is the evil that makes salvation relevant to begin with, if it is God's eternal purpose alone that will sustain us all the way, if our Christianity is all according to Scripture and not our brainstorms, all of grace and not our merits, all by faith and not by demands, all thanks to Christ and no thanks to us, all for the glory of God alone—where does our self-exaltation fit into that picture? <u>On the other hand, a heart at rest in our gracious Lord of glory, a heart at peace with other Christians who disagree with us—*that* is the heart of a true Calvinist.</u>

John Newton, the eighteenth-century Calvinist composer of "Amazing Grace," wisely wrote to a younger pastor, "Of all people who engage in controversy, we, who are called Calvinists, are most expressly bound by our own principles to the exercise of gentleness and moderation."

Jeff understands and embodies that. He himself has taken the journey that many of us are on—a journey from the child's play of theological arrogance to the sweetly humbled faith that true Calvinism calls for. Jeff has been led by grace into the green pastures and beside the still waters of true Calvinism, and this book can help us all to get there and stay there, in that place where the Lord himself is wonderfully present.

As a Calvinist, I rejoice in these striking evidences of God's favor on our generation—The Gospel Coalition, Together For The Gospel, the Acts 29 church-planting network, Reformed hip-hop and poetry, for starters.

Now may the Lord add, as the crowning beauty upon us all, humility, gentleness, kindness, and restraint, with a relaxed, cheerful enjoyment of one another. The modern rediscovery of Reformed theology, rather than leaving people cold, could then grow into historic revival, for the glory of God alone.

Ray Ortlund, Immanuel Church, Nashville
December 2018

1. THE PROBLEM WITH CALVINISM

What do you think is Calvinism's biggest weakness? I don't think it's the doctrines, or the points, or Calvin himself.

I think it's Calvinists like me.

Let's pretend God gives you a vision of heaven, lasting around ninety minutes or so.[1] You don't see unicorns or find out who shot JFK, but you see Jesus—and he's thrilled to see you. He takes you on a tour of his Father's house and the many rooms he promised to prepare for his brothers and sisters.

You walk by one wing of the Father's house. It's noisy, with lots of clapping and loud singing. Towering 20-foot-tall

---

1 Not how you imagined a book on Calvinism would begin? Me neither, but hang in there. It is pretend, after all.

double doors are open, and you and fellow saints redeemed by the blood of the Lamb wave and greet each other as you walk past. You ask Jesus, "What's going on in there?"

And Jesus tells you, "My charismatic family is having a little get-together."

"Ah," you say as you look back at them. "They seem like fun." Jesus nods.

The Lord leads you down another wing. This one is librarian-approved quiet. You hear a few laughs, but they're reserved ones. There's singing, but again, no one would accuse them of breaking any noise ordinances. Those towering doors? Open here too. You wave and greet brothers and sisters in Christ. The Anglicans, Methodists, and even some Baptists are meeting in this wing.

Twelve minutes left in your vision. Jesus takes you quickly through one more wing. Those doors? Closed. Jesus even begins to tiptoe down the hall, so, of course, you imitate him.

Jesus gives you the universal sign—index finger over the lips—to be quiet as you go. But you can't help yourself. "Jesus, why are the gigantic doors closed, and why are we being so quiet? Who's in there?"

"Well," the Lord explains, "the Calvinists are in there, and they think they are the only ones here. I'd hate to spoil it for them."

Now, this story is complete make-believe (you knew that, right?), and a very poor illustration of the perfect unity and fellowship we'll have in heaven—but it does highlight a problem with Calvinism. The problem is not Calvinism. It's Calvinists.

Here is the truth—my central thesis, if you like, and the starting point for this book. Many of us who love to love the "doctrines of grace" have not grown in showing grace. We have not become more gracious, kind, tender, and compassionate. And that can only mean one thing: we actually don't know the doctrines of grace. Sure, we know the points and can rehearse the arguments and even recall verses to support the five petals of our TULIP.[2] But an arrogant and argumentative Calvinist is just a Pharisee with a fresh coat of paint.

HOW CALVINISM FED MY IDOLS

I have a past. And I'm not proud of it. It's not my past before I became a Christian; it's my past *after* I became a Calvinist. For years, I carried around a Calvinism in which Jesus was, for the most part, ignored. My Calvinism was filled with data, puffed-up-ness, systematically arranged verses, talking points, arguments, anger, and quotes from Puritans. And sadly, I know I'm not alone.

---

2 Two pages in, and we've already had a decent amount of jargon— Calvinists, charismatic, TULIP... and there's some more to come. So if you want a brief explanation, turn ahead to page 31, where you'll find a brief interlude, and then just turn back to here. Feel free—it'll all still be here when you get back.

We all have various entry points into the doctrines of grace. For me, I was fifteen years old when my Sunday School teacher at a Reformed Baptist Church decided to teach us the five points of Calvinism. Until that point, Klein was the only Calvin I knew.

As the weeks and points unfolded, I didn't buck, fight, or shudder—it was like hearing Stevie Ray Vaughan play *Little Wing*. Riff after riff, I savored.

But something was off.

I salivated when I learned that many Christians disagree with some of the points. My knuckles cracked; theological taekwondo training had begun, and I was advancing beyond my peers. I had the arguments of Romans 9 primed and ready to sweep the leg of anyone who showed a hint of doubt or disagreement over predestination. Stack up the boards, I'll break them all. Upgrade my belt, Sensei.

I loved my Calvinism because it fed my pride and power; it kept the lights on in the idol factory. The gears in my head were turning, but my heart was jammed. A doctrinal disconnect between the head and heart fires up the production line of idolatry.

Via Calvinism, my pride idol was being met: "I've got Calvin and Spurgeon on my side. You better get on my side too. *I am right*." The power idol was in full swing: "I'll show them what they don't know. I know the truth. They need me." My approval idol was threatened: "How could you not agree with me—I mean, with this point of Calvinism?" When our idols get threatened or they get the opportunity to trounce others, they show their teeth and attack.

Maybe you've heard of a cage-stage Calvinist—someone who just learned about Calvinism and now needs to be locked in a cage so they don't whirl around like the Tasmanian Devil on *Looney Tunes*, harming the faith, hope, and love of everyone in their path. As the saying goes: it's just a stage. It'll pass.

But I'm not sure it always does pass.

I'm not so sure we don't often need to be caged whenever we meet a Christian who sees things a little different than we do.

I'm not sure many of us aren't carrying our cages around with us.

I'm not sure many of us can't tell that we're still behind bars.

And I want to eliminate the cage stage altogether.

The danger of the cage stage is that we often can't tell if we need to be locked up. We can't see the bridges we are burning because we are too busy breaking people's knees with theological arguments, wielding our Calvinism like a lead pipe. It often takes a rubble of relationships for us to see our cage-worthiness. And it usually takes a bold and courageous friend to tell us the error of our ways.

I needed those friends; and I still do. I recently sold my condo in Cage-Stage County—but, if I'm honest, I'm still tempted to drive around my old stomping grounds, looking for trouble. I still need those friends to help me chill out when the cage stage woos me back to the thug life of Calvinism. Not every not-Calvinistic-enough worship song needs my correction. Not every social media post from my Uncle Warner means I have to pick up my digital hammer, proclaiming, "Here I stand. I can do no other." (Luther said that first. He wasn't a Calvinist, but then, he would've been if he'd had the chance, right?) Beloved, since when did grace arm us against each other, rather than disarm us?

The eighteenth-century pastor, hymn-writer, and Calvinist John Newton kindly grilled and shish-kabobbed this breed of wise-headed-but-proud-hearted Calvinism in a letter to a friend:

> "I pity such wise-headed Calvinists as you speak of. I am afraid there are no people more fully answer the character, and live in the spirit of the Pharisees of old, than some professed loud sticklers for free grace. They are wise in their own eyes; their notions, which the pride of their hearts tells them are so bright and clear, serve them for a righteousness, and they trust in themselves and despise others.

> "One modest, inquiring Arminian is worth a thousand such Calvinists in my esteem."[3]

---

3 John Newton and Richard Cecil, *The Works of John Newton,* Vol. 6, page 197.

Proud Calvinism is a relevant threat in our time because Calvinism is hip again. It's cool to be a Calvinist. Even *Time Magazine*, back in 2009, saw New Calvinism as one of the top ten ideas changing the world.[4] The Young, Restless, and Reformed movement has been in full swing for over a decade. Ministries like The Gospel Coalition, Desiring God, and Together for the Gospel—and their respective mega-conferences—seem to expand more and more each year. And with great growth comes great responsibility. The danger we face in the midst of the swell is to think that Calvinists are winning the battle, or the popularity contest, or the godliness gala. But it's not meant to be about us versus them. It's not about winning. We've been picking the wrong battles.

PUFFING UP VS. BUILDING UP

Calvinism in the head will puff you up. Calvinism in the heart will build others up.

The apostle Paul warned some of the Corinthian believers about a potential source of arrogance: knowing that discounted meat in the marketplace was not ruined just because it had been offered to idols:

> "About eating food sacrificed to idols, then, we know that 'an idol is nothing in the world,' and that 'there is no God but one.' For even if there are so-called gods, whether in heaven or on earth—as there are many

---

4 http://content.time.com/time/specials/packages/article/
0,28804,1884779_1884782_1884760,00.html

'gods' and many 'lords'— yet for us there is one God, the Father. All things are from him, and we exist for him. And there is one Lord, Jesus Christ. All things are through him, and we exist through him."

(1 Corinthians 8 v 4-6)

The idols are nothing, said Paul. *Jesus is Lord. Eat away.*

However, some Corinthian saints, recognizing the cut of meat or knowing the butcher, would connect the dots to whichever idol's temple the meat came from and could then be tempted to worship idols. So Paul continues, "However, not everyone has this knowledge. Some have been so used to idolatry up until now that when they eat food sacrificed to an idol, their conscience, being weak, is defiled" (1 Corinthians 8 v 7). Those believers shouldn't buy it, grill it, or eat it. And the non-tempted believers, those who know the meat is just meat, *must not flaunt their knowledge:*

"Now about food sacrificed to idols: We know that 'we all have knowledge.' Knowledge puffs up, but love builds up. If anyone thinks he knows anything, he does not yet know it as he ought to know it."

(1 Corinthians 8 v 1-2)

What matters is not just knowing something, but knowing how to love someone.

Corinthian meat markets and Calvinism have a lot in common. When knowing isn't tethered to loving, helium happens. We get overinflated. Our pride's PSI rises, lifting us over others and pushing others aside because they don't know like we know. On the other hand, if we know the doctrines of grace in our hearts, and not just our heads, love results.

Here is the problem: the disconnect between our hearts and our heads. The distance from our heart to our head isn't far physically, but theologically the two are often far too far apart. Knowing the five points, the debating points, and the handy Spurgeon quotes in your head and not your heart will puff you up. But a heart-grasp of Calvinism yields a love that loves others and builds them up rather than a pride that loves looking down on others and tearing them down. Heart Calvinism helps us love the Lord our God with more than just our mind but with our heart, soul, and strength too. Heart Calvinism moves us to love our neighbors—all of them, not just our fellow Calvinists—as ourselves. Head Calvinism means we will become the kind of people who thrive on theological self-righteousness—the very people who received the harshest words from Jesus.

A LOVING CALVINISM

One of the fathers of "New Calvinism," John Piper, warns believers of the trap of loving the study of God more than God himself—loving learning more than the Lord himself. And there's also the danger of loving doctrine to the neglect of loving others. There is a fine line between rejoicing over the God we know and rubbing the doctrine we know in people's faces.

I know I've tripped on this line. I've been guilty of loving Calvinism rather than being a loving Calvinist. I've enjoyed the study of God and his ways more than the triune God himself. And if I know the five points, but do have not love, then I've got problems.

The famous love passage in 1 Corinthians 13 should inform the stride of every Christian. Paul's sweeping application of love isn't only to be read at weddings while everyone waits for cake. 1 Corinthians 13 is for life and ministry toward one another.

"If I speak human or angelic tongues but do not have love, I am a noisy gong or a clanging cymbal. If I have the gift of prophecy and understand all mysteries and all knowledge, and if I have all faith so that I can move mountains but do not have love, I am nothing. And if I give away all my possessions, and if I give over my body in order to boast but do not have love, I gain nothing." (1 Corinthians 13 v 1-3)

If we can speak eloquently about doctrine, but don't have love, we are like a feedbacking microphone or a phone ringing in the middle of a sermon. If we know a bucket of theological jargon, but don't have love, it's a big nothing-burger. Love matters.

I suspect a lot of people get turned off from Calvinism because of Calvinists. If you've been burned by us, I'm sorry. If you've been put off by what Calvinism teaches because you've seen how some Calvinists speak and act, then I understand. Calvinists like me get a rush of adrenaline over winning an argument or justifying our beliefs, and we tend to forget about loving our brothers and sisters who have also been justified by Christ. And that's wrong. In fact, the act of writing this chapter reminded me of a brother I needed to go back to and ask for his forgiveness. "I'm sorry for the way I handled our doctrinal disagreement. I was a jerk—unkind, impatient. Please, forgive me." He forgave me. We hugged. Laughed again. It was a glorious moment of gospel unity. If you love the five points, but you have allowed or even caused a rift with a brother or sister in Christ, it's time to go and make things right. You won't regret it. Pick up the phone now if you must. I'll wait.

If you are a Calvinist and you think I'm being unfair or unkind in my characterization of our tribe, I just want to ask you to look in the mirror with me. When people have been left unconvinced by my explanation of Calvinism, I'm tempted to think they don't care about the Bible, they don't take God's sovereignty seriously, and they are disrespecting grace. But what's more likely is that they walked away unconvinced because I didn't care about them, I didn't take the fruit of the Spirit seriously, and I disrespected grace by being ungracious. Could it be that your confidence in the Scriptures has ever come off as arrogance? Or that your zeal looked like impatience? Let's be known for our love.

CALVINISTS ARE...
Paul tells us in 1 Corinthians what Christ-infused love looks like toward one another, toward all Christians—not

just the ones who are like us in theology, or denomination, or skin-color, or anything else:

> "Love is patient, love is kind. Love does not envy, is not boastful, is not arrogant, is not rude, is not self-seeking, is not irritable, and does not keep a record of wrongs. Love finds no joy in unrighteousness but rejoices in the truth. It bears all things, believes all things, hopes all things, endures all things." (1 Corinthians 13 v 4-7)

We should be able to replace the word "love" with our own names. "Jeff is patient, Jeff is kind. Jeff does not envy." It's a great way to discover, with the Spirit's help, how loving or unloving we are toward others.

So, how about we put *Calvinists* in there?

> "Calvinists are patient, Calvinists are kind. Calvinists do not envy, Calvinists are not boastful, they are not arrogant, they are not rude, they are not self-seeking, Calvinists are not irritable, and they do not keep a record of wrongs. Calvinists find no joy in unrighteousness but rejoice in the truth. Calvinists bear all things, believe all things, hope all things, endure all things."

Did you wince, shake your head, or say *ouch, yeesh,* or *woof* out loud? 1 Corinthians 13 should be a description of Calvinists because it is a description of Christian love. But take the popular and—for good reason—negative stereotype of the common Calvinist, and how many of the loving qualities listed above are true? Maybe two:

"Calvinists find no joy in unrighteousness but rejoice in the truth." Since I've taken a Hebrew quiz in seminary before, I know two out of fifteen is a failing grade.

John Calvin, who knew a thing or two about Calvinism, tells us why we operate this way:

"Whence come rudeness, pride, and disdainful language towards brethren? Whence come quarrels, insults, and reproaches? Come they not from this, that every one carries his love of himself, and his regard to his own interests, to excess?"[5]

We are all prone to loving our theology, opinions, insights, and interests to excess. The scales are tipped. But grace can tip them back. More than merely loving Calvinism, we need a loving Calvinism. We don't need less Calvinism; we need real Calvinism—one that resides in our hearts rather than merely lodging in our heads.

NO ASTERISKS, NO FOOTNOTES

Rejoicing in the truth is important—but it doesn't give a free pass to impatience and arrogance. We may love rejoicing in the truth, but if we are unkind, our pants are on fire.

The apostle John reminds us that if we love God—even if our love for him has grown because of what we've learned in TULIP—and we belittle another Christian, we are fooling no one but ourselves:

---

5 John Calvin and William Pringle, *Commentaries on the Epistles of Paul to the Galatians and Ephesians*, page 267.

"We love because he first loved us. If anyone says, 'I love God,' and yet hates his brother or sister, he is a liar. For the person who does not love his brother or sister whom he has seen cannot love God whom he has not seen." (1 John 4 v 19-20)

Our love for God is questionable if we are unloving to one another. And by one another, John does not mean fellow five-pointers (or four, because, y'know, we're generous.) No—he means all God's children. All Christians.

You'll hear of people arriving at a "Reformed" view of salvation or subscribing to the five points of Calvinism in TULIP as coming to the "Reformed faith." I'm not a fan of this phrase because there is no Reformed faith, but only one Christian faith, as Paul lays out in Ephesians 4 v 4-6:

"There is one body and one Spirit—just as you were called to one hope at your calling—*one Lord, one faith, one baptism, one God and Father of all,* who is above all and through all and in all." (my italics)

And since there is all of this oneness, Paul urges us to live "with all humility and gentleness, with patience, bearing with one another in love, making every effort to keep the unity of the Spirit through the bond of peace" (Ephesians 4 v 2-3). There are no asterisks, footnotes, or yeah-buts to our unity in Christ. Jesus' blood runs deeper than temporary theological differences.

When we ramp up our theological differences, passing over all of our unity, we begin to divide from the inside.

We overlook humility, forgo kindness, shorten our fuses, and give up on putting up with one other; and we don't prioritize or pursue legitimate efforts at staying unified because we think our differences matter more than our oneness. We are wrong.

IS JOHN WESLEY IN HEAVEN?

I heard a story about when the eighteenth-century preacher George Whitefield, a vibrant Calvinist, was asked if he thought he would see the founder of the Methodists and well-known Arminian, John Wesley, in heaven.

Whitefield's answer? "No, I don't think we will."

Shocking, huh? But George wasn't done yet. He wouldn't see Wesley in heaven, he added, because, "Mr. Wesley will be so near the throne and I will be so far in the back that I will not be able to see him."

Humble Calvinism. Heart Calvinism. One Lord. One Faith. United above their differences.

The comments of the great Victorian preacher C.H. Spurgeon on this story of Whitefield and Wesley are insightful:

> "As I read such remarks made by Mr. Whitefield, I have said to myself, 'By this I know, as a Christian, that he must be a Christian'; for I saw that he loved his brother Wesley even while he so earnestly differed from him on certain points of doctrine. Yes, dear brethren, if we cannot differ, and yet love one

another—if we cannot allow each brother to go his own way in the service of God, and to have the liberty of working after his own fashion—if we cannot do that, we shall fail to convince our fellow-Christians that we ourselves are Christians."[6]

Love for one another, not Calvinism, is the way people know we are disciples of the risen Nazarene. "By this everyone will know that you are my disciples, if you love one another" (John 13 v 35). While we can't imitate the ministry, preaching, or smarts of Whitefield, all of us can imitate this style of Calvinism.

Spurgeon and Whitefield were not weak Calvinists. They were meek Calvinists. They didn't belittle the doctrines of grace, and they refused to belittle the Body or beat up their brethren. I wish I could say I always did the same.

SO, IS TODAY'S CALVINISM A LOST CAUSE?

Paul tells us the kind of posture we must have around the world and each other: "The Lord's servant must not quarrel, but must be gentle to everyone, able to teach, and patient, instructing his opponents with gentleness" (2 Timothy 2 v 24-25). Timothy is facing real opponents in Ephesus—unbelievers and false teachers—and you'd think Paul would say, "Let 'em have it." He doesn't. Paul says to take a different approach. Be patient and gentle to all—which does mean "all" here—and teach those

---

6 C.H. Spurgeon, "Christ's 'New Commandment,'" in *The Metropolitan Tabernacle Pulpit Sermons*, Vol. 51, page 249.

who disagree with gentleness. If gentleness is required for interacting with opponents outside of the church, we definitely shouldn't growl at one another inside the church over the doctrines of grace.

But why does this even happen? <u>Why do we act contrary to the grace we proclaim?</u> Well, it's not that Calvinism is damaged goods. It's that we are. We know, don't we, that we are sinners—and Paul showed us back in that Corinthian meat market what happens when sinners gain knowledge. Without love, it puffs up and tears down. We know in our heads but we need to know in our hearts.

So that's where this book is headed. We are going to crack open the five points, not so we can learn how to take down the opposition but so we can see what happens when the points get into our hearts. I am not arguing that we should shut down talking to others about the five points, or stop trying to show others what we believe about the mechanics of redeeming grace. It's in the Bible, and everything that is in the Bible "is profitable for teaching, for rebuking, for correcting, for training in righteousness, so that the man of God may be complete, equipped for every good work" (2 Timothy 3 v 16-17). But I *am* calling for us to see if these truths are in our hearts as well as our heads.

The reason we Calvinists often lack humility and a holy happiness is because we actually aren't beholding grace. We've studied the doctrines of grace but forgot the grace of God. I've done it. I've looked up the proof texts of each point of TULIP and looked right past Jesus, who is the grace of God (Titus 2 v 11). And a Christ-forgetting Calvinism produces the infamous cruel Calvinist. But real Calvinism, the Christ-enjoying Calvinism, creates humble and happy Calvinists. When we behold the glory of Jesus in the five points, our hearts burn within us, transforming us into the character of Christ: humble, lowly, kind, patient, loving.

We must see Christ in our Calvinism. If we don't, throw the tulips out; they are worthless. The love of Christ outclasses knowing raw Calvinistic data. Paul prays that believers would "know Christ's love that surpasses knowledge" (Ephesians 3 v 19). Nothing compares to the love of Christ. And when Calvinism makes known the love of Christ, a thunderclap of grace topples us back down and leaves us in awe of God's grace.

So, if you're reading this as a convinced Calvinist, I hope this book throws a few grenades your way. If you've rejected Calvinism because of what you've experienced of Calvinists, or you picked up this book because "humble" and "Calvinism" seemed strange words to find together, I pray it will be a balm to you. And if you're reading this and you are just coming across this thing called Calvinism, I hope it will serve as an introduction to the famous "five points." But, more than that, far more than that, I hope this book will show you what heart Calvinism—humble Calvinism, real Calvinism—looks like. Let's begin.

A SHORT INTERLUDE ABOUT JARGON AND HISTORY

One thing I know about Calvinists, two you can count on: they love theological jargon and church history. And, if you are anything like me, maybe you have used some of the terms without actually knowing what they mean, or mentioned some of the famous names without knowing who they are, but everyone else was doing the same and it seemed best to play along. If you are wondering if Calvin's favorite flowers were tulips, or why "Reformed" and "Reformation" seem not quite to mean the same thing—no worries. I've been there too. So, before we go any further in this book, let's get our ducks, definitions, and doctrine in a row. (And if you are totally up with the terminology and the historical highlights, feel free to skip this interlude and pass straight on to Chapter Two.)

ENTER PROTESTANTS

What came to be known as the Reformation began, pretty much, when a German monk named Martin Luther nailed a list of some controversial ideas about how we are saved to a door in Wittenberg, Germany, in 1517. (This was how you started a debate in those days—it's kind of like today's equivalent of writing a blog or writing to the New York Times.) Luther and a cast of "Reformers" throughout Europe challenged the Catholic Church on its views of salvation. Works-based salvation—the view that you contribute to your salvation with your own deeds—had come to dominate the preaching and practice of the church. The Reformers rallied and united around five *solas*, five "alones": Scripture alone, grace alone, faith alone, Christ alone, and God's glory alone.

Those who followed Luther's lead, believing that salvation is by grace alone, through faith in Christ—rather than by works—and that God speaks through the Bible—rather than through the church's interpretation of the Bible and its traditions—were (and are) "Protestant." They were so named because they were protesting against the dominant teaching of the Catholic Church (which, in western Europe at that time, was the only church in town).

John Calvin comes along in the story a little after Luther and his hammer. A Frenchman, Calvin became convinced by the teachings of the first generation of Reformers, and he too began to teach what had been rediscovered in the Reformation. Calvin was a gifted theologian, writer, and pastor-teacher. Calvin's ministry took root in Geneva, Switzerland, after he left Paris when the persecution there began to heat up. To cut a very long story far too short, in 1536 a friend persuaded him to set up shop in Geneva, where he could lead the church, write, preach, lecture, and (as it turned out) change Europe.

CALVIN DIDN'T INVENT CALVINISM

Now, the teachings of Calvinism existed long before Calvin entered the pulpit. Calvin didn't invent them. The Reformation revived the teachings of God's sovereign grace to save sinners. The "doctrines of grace," or "the five points of Calvinism," or "TULIP" go like this:

- Total Depravity: We are totally unrighteous and need God to save us.

- Unconditional Election: God chose to save sinners apart from any human merit.

- Limited Atonement: Jesus' death on the cross secured the salvation specifically of his people.

- Irresistible Grace: Sinners believe in Christ because God draws them to himself.

- Perseverance of the Saints: Christians cannot lose their salvation; they will endure till the end.

Calvin taught much more than Calvinism. In his day, he would have scoffed at the idea of an "–ism" being tethered to his name. In the *Institutes of the Christian Religion*—his major work of theology—you'll find more pages devoted to prayer, baptism, and the Lord's Supper than to election. Calvin wouldn't have been obsessed with what is called Calvinism, and nor was he the only one to promote its truths; other Reformers like Zwingli, Bucer, and Cranmer taught the doctrines of grace too.

Calvin (like the others named in that last sentence) didn't agree with Luther on everything—perhaps most notably, on the Lord's Supper and what should happen in church services. Those who lined up (for the most part) with Calvin became known—somewhat confusingly— as "Reformed"—while those who lined up (for the most part) with Luther and his wingman Philip Melanchthon were called (more sensibly) "Lutherans." So, ironically, the man who began the Reformation is known as a Reformer, but wouldn't be described as "Reformed" by his tribe. Confusing? I know.

Calvin is likely best known for the five points—for TULIP. Yet Calvin didn't design this floral arrangement. Acronyms weren't all the rage in the 1500s like they were in the 1900s—and Calvin didn't write in English either. David Murray, an author and professor at Puritan Reformed Theological Seminary, says that the TULIP acronym first appeared in 1932, in the book *The Reformed Doctrine of Predestination* by Loraine Boettner.[7] And then TULIP gained more traction from the 1963 book(let) *The*

---

7 http://headhearthand.org/blog/2015/10/12/theres-more-to-
calvinism-than-the-five-points-of-calvinism/

Five Points of Calvinism Defined, Defended and Documented by David Steele and Curtis Thomas.

Not only that, but Calvin didn't even come up with the five points. These five points weren't something people waved around all the time; they were actually a response to a group of people influenced by Jacob Arminius, a quiet dissenter to some of the Reformation's teachings. A year after Arminius's death in 1609, some Dutch Arminians presented a Remonstrance—a protest—to the Reformed Church of Holland, challenging the church's teaching on God's sovereignty and free will, unconditional predestination, and the power of grace. After eight years of arguing between Calvinism and Arminians, in 1618 the Synod of Dort was called, which is a fancy way to say a church meeting happened in Dordrecht in the Netherlands. (Dort is much kinder to the eyes.)

What went down at Dort was a rebuffing and rejection of the Remonstrance from the Arminians. The synod drafted a denial, organized in points that denied the five points of the Remonstrance and reaffirmed the already-held truths of the Reformed churches throughout Europe. And so Dort put forward what we know as the five points of Calvinism. But not everyone went for it. And ever since then, there have been Calvinists and Arminians,[8] and plenty of others who hold to one side or the other but

---

8 Well, the debate goes back even further to the 5th century and Augustine debating Pelagius, but ain't nobody got time for that in this section. (And anyway, plenty of Arminians wouldn't see themselves in agreement with Pelagius.)

don't use the labels, maybe because they don't like them, or because they've never heard of them. A difference of opinion over TULIP doesn't mean the difference between orthodoxy or heresy. Both camps are seeking to love God, take the Bible seriously, and see people love Jesus.

While the label "Calvinism" stuck, don't think it's because Calvin put his initials on the papers at Dort. Calvin had died a few years earlier and was already enjoying the presence of Christ. But Calvin's influence couldn't be denied. His God-centered, Bible-text-driven, grace-illumined teaching, preaching, and writing are why "Calvinist" theology took that name. And they are why (humanly speaking) it became one of the many streams in the Protestant river, flowing through the centuries in the writing and preaching of others like, in no particular order of importance or chronology, C.H. Spurgeon and John Newton, George Whitefield and Jonathan Edwards, Charles Simeon and Thomas Chalmers, and Puritans (English and Scottish Reformed guys in the late sixteenth and seventeenth centuries) such as John Owen and John Milton. While Calvinism contains much more than "the five points," it's certainly not less. TULIP, without question, is the most well-known aspect of Calvinism and Reformed theology, and it's what we will focus on throughout this book.

NEW CALVINISM

The reason you are reading a new book on Calvinism is because of what's been called "the New Calvinism," a resurgence in the focus on and popularity of Calvinism in the 21st century. Collin Hansen, Editorial Director at The Gospel Coalition, wrote a book tracing the revival of Calvinism titled, *Young, Restless, Reformed: A Journalist's Journey with the New Calvinists*. Collin's book came out in 2008. And Calvinism is still surging forward.

Calvinism is popular again in large part because of the teachings and writings of John Piper, R.C. Sproul, Matt Chandler, Tim Keller, J.I. Packer, Michael Horton, Tim Challies, and many more; and we can't overlook the influence of Reformed rap from Reach Records, Lamp Mode, and Humble Beast. Generations of new Calvinists have gleaned from the fields of ministries like Desiring God, Ligonier, The Gospel Coalition, Proclamation Trust, Newfrontiers, the Southern Baptist Theological Seminary, 9 Marks, the Acts 29 church-planting network and so on (if I left out your favorite—forgive me. This is meant to be a short chapter in a short book.) The resurgence of Calvinism has even created a phenomenon of bobbleheads (many of which I have), coffee mugs and t-shirts, rocking Reformed theology or showing some love for long-dead Calvinists. My study at our church office is filled with pictures of dead Reformers. My wife thinks it's creepy— hence the pictures being at the church office.

The ironic thing about New Calvinism is that its least-read long-dead Calvinist is probably Calvin. I'd bet my copy of Calvin's *Institutes* that Puritan paperbacks, Spurgeon, and John Piper fill the shelves of New Calvinists more than

Calvin does. Which is too bad, because Calvin's sermons are piercing, his commentaries are energetic and focused on Christ, and the *Institutes* shows you his passion for people to know and love God. But in a sense, it also doesn't matter too much, because Calvinism isn't about Calvin; it's about the teachings of God's word.

What makes New Calvinism stand out is that it's not restricted to Presbyterians or Baptists or any denomination. TULIP has taken root in many soils. Charismatics—those who believe that specific spiritual gifts like prophecy and healing are operational today—and non-charismatics—those who believe those gifts ended with the apostles—alike enjoy the God-soaked teachings of Calvinism. New Calvinism is an awakening of gospel-centered, mission-driven, theologically committed Christians, throughout the world.

That's enough history for today. Whether you are a Calvinist or not, you are now all caught up on the jargon, acronyms, and name-drops needed to enjoy this book—and to keep up with Calvinist conversations.

2. WHY HUMBLE CALVINISM ISN'T AN OXYMORON

G race. That's what's for dinner—and dessert. Brunch, too.

The food pyramid of the kingdom of heaven is grace upon grace. "Indeed, we have all received grace upon grace from his fullness" (John 1 v 16). Our plates are topped with heaped scoops of grace saddled next to thick-cut steaks of the marvelous grace of our loving God.

Grace is our greatest dietary need. Grace isn't a blob of Christian sentiments and manners. Grace is our Savior: "For the grace of God has appeared, bringing salvation for all people" (Titus 2 v 11). The grace of God is one of Jesus' nicknames. So, when I say grace is our dinner, our brunch, and our afternoon macchiato, I'm saying Jesus is our need and our nourishment.

Without Jesus, we can't do a single thing to bear fruit in our lives. Jesus says, "I am the vine; you are the branches. The one who remains in me and I in him produces much fruit, because you can do nothing without me" (John 15 v 5). It's no stretch to say that all of our faith's caloric energy and excitement comes from our gracious Redeemer, Jesus himself.

Think about the times Jesus tells us he's our food. Our bread: "I am the bread of life" (John 6 v 35). Our drink: "If anyone is thirsty, let him come to me and drink"(John 7 v 37). Jesus describes the menu more when he says, "Truly I tell you, unless you eat the flesh of the Son of Man and drink his blood, you do not have life in yourselves. The one who eats my flesh and drinks my blood has eternal life, and I will raise him up on the last day" (John 6 v 53-54). The Christian life is a feast of faith on Jesus. The faith once for all delivered to the saints is centered, nourished, satisfied, and joyfully fixated on Jesus—who he is, what he's done, what he is doing, and what he will do.

Now, you likely know all this, but do you *know* all this? It's easy to consume Calvinist doctrine without feasting on Christ. Let me ask you this: what subject is most likely to get you reading? Is it doctrine... controversy... Calvinism... or Christ?

Friends, we mustn't just feast on tulips. They're actually dangerous.

During the Second World War, as a food shortage hit the

German-occupied Netherlands, its citizens were starving. The desperate Dutch turned to one of their most famous products—the tulips. But there was a problem. While tulip bulbs can be edible, they are poisonous if they're undercooked. Netherlanders ate what they thought would be an answer to their problem, only to experience stomach pain, dizziness, and convulsions from eating undercooked tulip bulbs.

You know what's more dangerous than mishandled tulip bulbs? An undercooked TULIP—it has even nastier effects. And it's not like we have a shortage of food. Christ—not doctrine—is the bread of life. Our problem is we look for nutrition in petals rather than the bread and blood.

WHAT DO I ENJOY MORE?
When I got my first whiff of TULIP, it was a multi-sensory experience. Awe, delight, wonder, joy. I loved the smell and loved to tell others about the aroma. And because I memorized a slew of verses and theological jargon—and someone spotted the kernel of a teaching gift—it looked like I was mature enough for a church to hire me as their College Minister.

God used this magnificent mistake to redirect my heart and life.

As I sat in my closet-turned-office at the first church that hired me, I heard a sermon clip where the preacher wouldn't stop talking about Jesus. Literally, he talked about Jesus over and over. It arrested me.

I looked at my notes for my next sermon and a haunting chill came over me. The difference between my sermon and his was like raw chicken and crispy, golden-fried chicken. I was giving seminars on Calvinism; he was preaching Christ crucified and raised from the dead. I wasn't keeping the main thing the main thing. The gospel wasn't of first importance to me or my sermon, even though I thought it was.

Right at this time, the gospel-centered movement began to rise, and as books like *God is the Gospel* by John Piper and *Gospel Wakefulness* by Jared C. Wilson hit my hands, it became painfully clear that my passions were upside down.

I knew proof texts for TULIP better than I knew the four Gospels. I loved truths about God and his ways more than God. I knew Jesus died for me and rose for me, but I barely knew anything else about the one who loved me and gave himself for me—my sympathetic high priest, the one who's not ashamed to call me his brother, the one who lives to intercede for me. I needed to change.

HE LOVES ME

While I was still hopped up on Calvinism pills, God's word pierced my heart like a bunker-busting missile. For years, doctrine had been accumulating in my head, neatly organized and accessible. Theology was a mental exercise that never engaged my emotions. My affections were not stirred for Christ (though a good argument got my pulse racing). I spent my time reading the Bible to hunt doctrines, catch them, stuff them, and mount them on the wall of my mind. Theological taxidermy was my hobby.

Then one day, while on my habitual safari, Galatians 2 v 20 refused to be poached. It roared back at me in a comforting confrontation of gospel joy:

"I have been crucified with Christ, and I no longer live, but Christ lives in me. The life I now live in the body, I live by faith in the Son of God, who loved me and gave himself for me."

I became consumed by the radical implications of being crucified and risen with Christ. In fact, I became consumed by *Christ*. And that meant that he was no longer lost in the heavy fog of doctrine for doctrine's sake. Jesus' love became more real to me than ever before. I'd read the verse before, and I already knew the truths tucked in it—union with Christ, penal substitutionary atonement—but I *felt* the truths this time. The God-man from Nazareth, who sustains the cosmos with the word of his power, actually loves me.

Me.

He loves *me*.

He loves you too.

I began to hunt down and track the cross-references and wordings that were similar to Galatians 2 v 20, and it led me to one of the most powerful phrases in the New

Testament. In Colossians, Paul echoes Galatians 2 v 20 but adds another whoa factor when he says, "For you died, and your life is hidden with Christ in God. When *Christ, who is your life,* appears, then you also will appear with him in glory" (Colossians 3 v 3-4, my italics). *Christ, who is your life*—this is significant.

When people say, "My grandkids are my life," they mean their grandkids are everything to them: their life revolves around them; they spend their time and affections for those kids. When Olympians talk about their sport being their life, they mean it defines everything they do—their habits, schedules, training, diet; everything is seen through the lens of their sport, their life.

Are you this way with Christ?

Is *Christ, who is your life,* functionally, practically, noticeably true to you? Does your life revolve around Jesus? Does he define you? Is he everything to you? If he's not, what is?

Is it possible that some of us act like Calvinism—knowing it, debating it, proving it, defending it, teaching it, being defined by it—is our life? I used to. And if I'm not careful, I can easily fall back into thinking that Calvinism is my life. And that's no way to live when Christ is available.

God shows us in *Christ, who is your life* what is so obvious and yet so many of us miss: Christianity is all about Christ. Jesus isn't the mascot of Christianity—he is Christianity. Michael Reeves, author and theologian, captures this when he says:

"The center, the cornerstone, the jewel in the crown of Christianity is not an idea, a system, or a thing; it is not even 'the gospel' as such. It is Jesus Christ.

"He is not a mere topic, a subject we can pick out from a menu of options. Without him, our gospel or our system—however coherent, 'grace-filled' or 'Bible-based'—simply is not Christian. It will only be Christian to the extent that it is about him, and then what we make of him will govern what we mean by the word gospel. I'm going to dare to say, in fact, that most of our Christian problems and errors of thought come about precisely through forgetting or marginalizing Christ."[9]

Our Calvinism must be all about Christ. A Christ-less Calvinism is a tragedy—it's not even Christianity. Real Calvinism is a Christ-enthralled garden of grace. My hope for this book is that you'll see the points of Calvinism not as lights in which to bask but as a lit path toward enjoying Jesus, the light of the world, personally and powerfully.

BRAG ABOUT JESUS

The most important five-letter word in Calvinism isn't TULIP. It's Jesus. He has first place in everything (Colossians 1 v 18). The whole Bible is about him (John 5 v 39). The apostle Paul tells us again and again that our swagger must go and we are to boast only in the Lord. "So

9 Michael Reeves, *Rejoicing in Christ*, page 10.

let the one who boasts, boast in the Lord" (2 Corinthians 10 v 17). If we are going to toot a horn, there's one note we have: "But as for me, I will never boast about anything except the cross of our Lord Jesus Christ" (Galatians 6 v 14). Christ is our confidence. Christ is our cause. Christ is our song.

Let's brag about Jesus. Parents have no problems bragging on their kids: *Johnny did this at soccer... and you just won't believe what little Sally said the other day.* We brag about what we love.

You mind if I brag about the Lord for a minute? Join me.

Jesus literally holds the entire universe together, and yet he's never too busy for me. My Jesus walked on a Galilean sea, in the middle of a raging storm, and acted like it was no big deal. And another time, he told the wind and the waves that enough was enough: "Be still!" I can't even get my dog to sit.

In the town of Cana, a groom failed to bring enough wine for the wedding afterparty—a big embarrassing social no-no. Instead of running to the corner store, Jesus turned water into wine, showcasing his glory and his kindness for this failing newly-wed. Jesus helps failures. Jesus is there in crises.

Jesus is so kind to us that even when we are at our lowest, he still wants to keep us. Even when we wanted nothing to do with Jesus, he still wanted us. He still loved us. When I forget to ask Jesus for help, he still helps me.

The crowds mocked Jesus. So what? The Pharisees were always out to get him. No big deal. His family tried to get him to tone down his preaching. Fat chance. Jesus still hung out with the people that compromised his reputation. The people that society had kicked to the curb—Jesus went to them. He has a large heart for the outcasts, the misunderstood, the oddballs. He's the Messiah of the misfits.

When I hear a noise in my backyard at two in the morning, I just hope it's the neighborhood cat. Darkness and danger terrify me, but not Jesus. Our Lord went toe-to-toe with the demonic powers. Jesus stood up to these ancient bullies as they controlled and hurt men, women, and children. One command from Jesus and the demons scurried like roaches in the light.

Jesus encountered people with broken muscle tissue and misbehaving cellular structures, limbs, and organs. All fixed by the Carpenter of carpenters. The great Physician told a man with a shriveled and paralyzed hand to go ahead—stretch that arm out. Healed.

Jesus let Peter walk on water, contorting the sub-atomic properties of liquids and solids. And then he let Peter sink too, before enabling him to stand again. We'd all sink without Jesus.

Though fully God—not God junior, diet God, or bargain-basket God—Jesus really did let Roman soldiers nail iron spikes into his body. My Jesus did that for me. For my sins. Angels worship him, the universe depends on him, and he died for me.

Jesus became a cold corpse on a slab, but he refused to stay that way. He guaranteed he would rise from the dead and he did. His heart started pumping, his brainstem fired back on, and his central nervous system booted up. He lives. And he is alive in heaven, inviting us to go to him, to believe in him, to follow him, and to enjoy him.

When I'm unfaithful, he's faithful. When I'm clueless, he's patient. When I'm lost, he brings me back. When I'm confused, he's clarifying. When I'm forgetful, he's steady. Though there are times when I'm embarrassed to talk about him, he's not ashamed to call me his brother, friend, co-heir.

Every thought, inclination, and urge Jesus has is totally righteous—and we can't even begin to imagine that, because our thoughts, inclinations, and urges are so often totally not. In gym class, if Jesus had the first pick, he'd pick the kid who is always picked last, the kid we'd hope goes to the other team. We struggle to serve one another, grumbling as we get out of bed to make sure our spouse locked the front door; Jesus, however, with joy set before him, endured the cross to the point of death to save his Bride.

Jesus doesn't use an iron fist to lead us or intimidate us into following him. Jesus transforms us: he removes the blinders, and we see what the angels long to peer into.

Jesus is realistic about our abilities. We lose our keys and can't remember where we parked our car. There's no way we can manage our salvation. He keeps us. He's got us.

We could go on, but this book, even the world, can't contain all of the ways we could brag about our Lord (John 21 v 25). We need a kind of Calvinism that doesn't humblebrag about itself or about its footsoldiers, but loves to brag about the God of grace.

WHERE THE POINTS POINT

John Calvin shared this passion. He knew the mega-theme of the Bible is Jesus Christ. Not the sin of man, or predestination, or even the atonement—but Jesus himself:

> "This is what we should in short seek in the whole of Scripture: truly to know Jesus Christ, and the infinite riches that are comprised in him and are offered to us by him from God the Father. If one were to sift thoroughly the Law and the Prophets, he would not find a single word which would not draw and bring us to him ... It is therefore not lawful that we turn away and become diverted even in the smallest degree by this or that. On the contrary, our minds ought to come to a halt at the point where we learn in Scripture to know Jesus Christ and him alone, so that we may be directly led by him to the Father who contains in himself all perfection."[10]

---

10 Joseph Haroutunian and Louise Pettibone Smith, *Calvin: Commentaries*, page 70.

Jesus is the point of Calvinism because Jesus is the point of the Bible. Calvin's beard would curl if he knew an itemized list of doctrines—bearing his name!—had divided Christ's people and didn't lead us to know and enjoy Jesus Christ. The five points are meant to be five pointers—pointers to Jesus and his grace. In fact, the last five braggable truths about Jesus you just enjoyed—his inclination, his pick in gym class, and so on—were the points of TULIP, showcasing Jesus's incomparable glory.

Like C.H. Spurgeon, we should enjoy the points only when they are connected to Christ:

"How I do love the doctrines of grace when they are taken in connection with Christ. Some people preach the Calvinistic points without Jesus; but what hard, dry, marrowless preaching it is ... let every believer remember he does not get these doctrines as he should get them, unless he receives them in Christ."[11]

TULIP's aroma must be that of Christ. Christ-forgotten Calvinism is dry, rusty, lifeless. Without Jesus, Calvinism is nothing; it's a placebo of grace. But real Calvinism redirects our hearts to the glory of our Redeemer. We are sinful, Jesus isn't, but he became our sin to save us. We were chosen in Christ. Jesus loves us and died for our sins. We were drawn to believe in Christ because of God. We are saved forever in Christ. Christ-savoring Calvinism is soul food.

---

11 C.H. Spurgeon, "Alpha and Omega," in *The Metropolitan Tabernacle Pulpit Sermons*, Vol. 9, pages 715-716.

POINTING TO JESUS

Jumbo shrimp.

Long shorts.

Larger half.

Plastic glasses.

Freezer burn.

Pretty ugly.

Original copy.

Humble Calvinist?

The first time I mentioned the idea of writing a book on humble Calvinism, my friend laughed and said, "Humble Calvinism? Isn't that an oxymoron?" Given my own personal history, I couldn't disagree with him. Humble Calvinist sounds to many of us as oxymoronic as jumbo shrimp and freezer burn. But while it is often true in practice, it is not true in theory and should not be true in reality.

Real Calvinism is humble because real Calvinism is about Christ. And he is the definition of humble.

The purpose of the points is—or should be—to show us Jesus. And when we see Jesus and his love, we learn about him and from him. True Calvinism is necessarily humble. When we see the five points as five pointers to Jesus, we see him more clearly and ourselves more humbly. The greater God's grace in Jesus becomes to us, the more humble we become. Proud Calvinism is a moronic oxymoron. But real Calvinism is centered on Christ, humbling us because it brings us to the feet of Christ—where he's ready to wash our feet.

A Christ-centered Calvinism is a humble Calvinism because it's making us Christ-like. When Jesus says, "Learn from me, because I am lowly and humble in heart" (Matthew 11 v 29), the Lord opens his own heart and shows us what he is like: lowly and humble. And as the points of Calvinism open up the glory of Christ, Christ connects our hearts to his. He's teaching us to be like himself—lowly and humble. As Andrew Murray writes in his book, *Humility*, on the all-pervasive humility of Jesus:

"What is the incarnation but his heavenly humility; his emptying himself and becoming man? What is his life on earth but humility; his taking the form of a servant? And what is his atonement but humility? 'He humbled himself, and became obedient unto death' (Philippians 2 v 8). And what is his ascension and his glory, but humility exalted to the throne and crowned with glory?"[12]

If we learn the five points but don't learn humility from Jesus, we missed it. But we can get back on the path.

Jesus wants to teach us humility. He's already invited us into his school. Murray calls us to "study the character

---

12 Andrew Murray, *Humility*, page 14.

of Christ until our souls are filled with the love and admiration of his lowliness."[13] As we enjoy the glory of Jesus via the five points, we will be humbled, brought low, in awe of grace. We can all keep learning the way of humility from our kind Savior. Humility is what the doctrines of grace, when cooked thoroughly, are meant to produce in us. Humility before the Lord and one another. We need the nutrients of grace to get into our bloodstream—down into our hearts and not just our brains.

Now, it's time to put on our stretchy pants and enjoy a five-course feast of grace. The table is set. Let's eat.

---

13 *Humility,* page 7.

3. TOTAL DEPENDENCY

Disney World is already a nerve-racking place, but when your four-year-old may not meet the height requirements for the rides, it's desperation time.

My son couldn't wait to ride The Dinosaur, Test Track, and Star Tours—a Star Wars adventure—but his height was suspect. So, his parents did what parents do. My wife bought Oliver a pair of thick-soled Timberland boots and put him in an extra pair of socks. When the height-checker eye-balled Oliver, she asked him to come over and see if he measured up. The dutiful Disney employee deployed her canary yellow measuring stick—whose chipped paint hadn't kept it from crushing the dreams of many kids before. But my boy strutted up to his enemy and won.

My wife is a genius.

When it comes to entry into God's perfect presence, many of us, deep down, are deploying the same sneaky strategy.

But there's no duping God. No amount of smuggled-in extra socks of serving others or Timberlands of trying to be good people will give us the boost we need. Sin has stunted us, shortened us. All of us. Totally.

WHY WE NEED GRACE

The first point in the doctrines of grace sets the stage for our need of grace. Total Depravity tells us that we are totally unable to save ourselves, totally guilty and trapped by sin, and in need of a total overhaul.

But, don't you think the word "depraved" has too much bite to it? Isn't "sinner" enough? Well, let's not scrap the word just yet. There is a defense for the word "depravity."

By saying I'm a sinner, I'm admitting I've done some straying from God's commands. Not breaking news. But depravity means more than committing a few sins—it means my nature and will are corrupted. Sin's poison has permeated my whole person. Depravity means in Latin that we are *de*—down, or thoroughly—*pravus*—crooked or perverse. You and I are not people who stubbed our big toe on the cobblestone well of sin. We are people who jumped into the well and now lie in it with legs broken and no strength, trapped.

WIDE-ANGLE AND ZOOM

The "total" in Total Depravity highlights two things. First, the entire human race is in this shipwreck. No exemptions. Nobody lucked out and got the genes to ward off anger, lust, and all the other sins we all know too well. No race, gender, or generation has better odds at muscling out of sin's slums. You won't land anywhere on this earth and find an innocent tribe or family, just living their lives perfectly without any depravity. The apostle Paul is clear:

> "For we have already charged that both Jews and Gentiles are all under sin, as it is written: There is no one righteous, not even one. There is no one who understands; there is no one who seeks God. All have turned away; all alike have become worthless. There is no one who does what is good, not even one."
>
> (Romans 3 v 9-12)

We'd never turn to God on our own because we don't even know we need him. Our depravity blinds us from seeing our depravity. *Total* Depravity means *everyone* is corrupted by sin and needs God to grant his pardoning mercy.

The second totality of Total Depravity switches from wide-angle to zoom. Individually, we are depraved—right down to the core control center of our beings. Jesus said, "For from the heart come evil thoughts, murders, adulteries, sexual immoralities, thefts, false testimonies, slander" (Matthew 15 v 19). We sin because we are born with hearts that are sinful, lawless, pre-loaded with depravity. We can't shatter the shackles of our sin—and apart from God's intervention, we don't *want* them smashed. "The mind-set of the flesh is hostile to God because it does not submit to God's law. Indeed, it is unable to do so. Those who are in the flesh cannot please God" (Romans 8 v 7-8).

Our depraved default nature means that we are unable to obey God—and that we don't even want to.

Sin is when we live like the most relevant reality in the universe is irrelevant, ignorable, and even idiotic. It's missing the mark of God's glory. "For all have sinned and fall short of the glory of God" (Romans 3 v 23). We've come up short—infinitely short; and God's not a Disney World employee who can be fooled by a bit of standing straight in the power of high self-esteem and wearing extra spiritual socks of church attendance, good doctrine, or making sure that (in our own, not unbiased, assessment) our good outweighs our bad.

In *Terminator 2*, Arnold Schwarzenegger plays an android sent from the future to protect a young boy, John Connor, from a cyborg assassin who wants to kill John before he can lead humanity against the world-destroying Skynet AI. (Stay with me.) One day, as John watches children fighting and yelling at each other, he asks Arnie (the Terminator), "We're not gonna make it, are we? People, I mean." The Terminator answers, "It's in your nature to destroy yourselves." In response to which young John laments, "Yeah. Major drag, huh?"

The Terminator was theologically on point. He's summing up total depravity. It's in our nature to destroy ourselves and one another with sin. Left on our own, we'd burn the world down. Paul tells us in Ephesians 2 the truth about who we are. It's not pretty:

"And you were dead in your trespasses and sins in which you previously lived according to the ways of this world, according to the ruler of the power of the air, the spirit now working in the disobedient. We too all previously lived among them in our fleshly desires, carrying out the inclinations of our flesh and thoughts, and we were by nature children under wrath as the others were also." (Ephesians 2 v 1-3)

Depravity is a death certificate—we are spiritual corpses. The Bible doesn't paint a picture of us as being basically good people needing a nudge in the right direction. We are intrinsically sinful people needing a rescue from wrath.

HANDLE WITH CARE

It's important to remember what Total Depravity *isn't* saying. While everything we do is tainted by our sinfulness, Total Depravity does not mean that we are always, or even ever, as bad as we could be. It also doesn't teach that human beings never do anything good for one another.

I've been guilty of overreacting to the word "good." When someone would say, "Man, he's a good guy," I'd think to myself, "No one is good. No, not one. Don't you know about total depravity?" But we have no problem saying "He's a good preacher" or "She's a good writer" without fear of a fellow Calvinist slapping us with a violation of Romans 3. These are qualified, subjective, relative "goods." Good parent, good friend, good neighbor, good employee—all of us, including unbelievers, can be these things, via the common grace of God's blessings to all people.

Australian theologian Michael Bird is right when he says:

"The point affirmed in total depravity is not a denial of this human capacity for good; rather, it is an affirmation that sin totally permeates our intellect, wills, and hearts. There is no cavern of our mind, no recess of our soul, and no room of our heart that is not infected with the deadly virus of sin."[14]

Holding the door open for an elderly woman is a good thing to do. We're free to recognize, praise, and celebrate the doing of good in this world. Helping the least of these in the world is good. It's just not good enough to save you or to cancel out or overcome your depravity.

NO LONGER TOTALLY, SORT OF

So far, so dead-in-sin. But of course God did not leave us there. Ephesians 2 famously continues, "But God..." Christians were born totally depraved but have been born again into total forgiveness and salvation. We have been made totally new. So, are believers still depraved? Totally? Well, no. And yes, kinda.

On this side of eternity, in Christ, we are not either-or; we are both-and. As Martin Luther said, "A Christian man is both righteous and a sinner, holy and profane, an enemy of God

---

14 Michael F. Bird, *Evangelical Theology: A Biblical and Systematic Introduction*, page 675.

and yet a child of God."[15] We are *simul iustus et peccator*—simultaneously justified and righteous before God and yet still battling sin and sometimes failing to resist it.

We are declared righteous in Christ, but we don't always live righteously. We battle temptation, confess when we sin, and enjoy the forgiveness God promises us in the risen Son (1 John 1 v 9). We are no longer dead in our depravity but are alive to God in Christ (Romans 6 v 6-11). Our good works, in Christ, are no longer filthy self-righteous rags, "For we are his workmanship, created in Christ Jesus for good works, which God prepared ahead of time for us to do" (Ephesians 2 v 10). We are no longer only totally depraved. We have hope—and we have no excuse. The Christian can never shrug at their sin and say, "Hey, I'm just totally depraved, remember?" The doctrine of depravity is not a get-out-of-rebuke card to lay down. In Christ, you aren't only totally depraved anymore. You are new.

Isn't this your experience? We want to follow Christ—we want to honor him, and love our neighbors; and yet we bumble it again and again. We struggle to do what we want to do, and often do what we don't want to do. We are sinner-saints. But the good news of the gospel is that while depravity often describes us, it no longer defines us; we are now totally identified with Jesus. He's growing us. He's leading us. He's got us. We are already distanced from our depravity—but not totally, not yet. We haven't arrived.

---

15 Martin Luther, *Commentary on Galatians*, page 226.

And because we are always accompanied in this life by depravity, we should always be marked by a deep humility. Until the day I die, my indwelling, ongoing sin will remind me that my future beyond death, my depravity-free eternity, was not earned by me. It was given to me. I won't strut into the New Jerusalem. Christ will carry me in. There's only one set of footprints in the sand. My friend Jared C. Wilson comically spoofs the poem about the single set of footprints in the sand, by imagining God saying to us, "My child, there's only ever been one set of footprints in the sand, because your sorry butt has always needed to be carried."[16] This knowledge will defeat pride every day of my life.

Or at least it should. But—because of my depravity—it often doesn't.

STOP SPECK-SPOTTING

When we have a mind-alone understanding of the sinful nature of humanity, all kinds of unsavory attitudes and actions spill out. For me, instead of thinking humbly of the sinner right here—the one writing this chapter—a head-grasp of total depravity points me to all those nasty sinners out there.

Jesus called out this speck-spotting. And Calvinists tend to be really good at this:

"Why do you look at the splinter in your brother's

---

16 https://twitter.com/jaredcwilson/status/628920068500402176

eye, but don't notice the beam of wood in your own eye? Or how can you say to your brother, 'Brother, let me take out the splinter that is in your eye,' when you yourself don't see the beam of wood in your eye? Hypocrite! First take the beam of wood out of your eye, and then you will see clearly to take out the splinter in your brother's eye." (Luke 6 v 41-42)

It seems like Reformed sport these days to go sniffing for other people's sins. We can identify people's idols, talk about the sin beneath the sin, and point out legalism in others. Like bloodhounds, we can smell doctrinal error 130 miles away. We notice other people's micro-splinters while looking past our own eye-timber with "Depravity" spray-painted on the side. But real Calvinism means we remember the lumber dangling from our eye sockets.

The times when we believe we are better than our brothers and sisters in Christ, because we don't sin or struggle like they do, we believe our own propaganda. We hit the power button on the personal hype-machine of our hearts—but the fine print reads, "Hypocrite."

So OK, you don't have an anger problem like the guy in your small group, but have you forgotten about your gluttony? OK, you don't battle same-sex attraction like the gal in your accountability group—but how's your envy and coveting going? Are you are hiding a pornography addiction while you lecture your friend about always being late? We are so good at looking past the existence of our planks while feeling proud that we don't struggle with others' specks.

Jesus isn't saying to mind our own business and not exhort one another. He's saying to mind ours first. Our lumber yard keeps us humble among the saints. When the doctrine of Total Depravity enters our heads but not our hearts, we end up, without really noticing, applying it to everyone on earth except ourselves. But we can't connect other people's sins to their Total Depravity, and then blame our rudeness on a sleepless night, or our irritability to a lack of coffee. Well, we can—but the fine print still reads, "Hypocrite."

Jesus tells a powerful parable about two men praying—one knows about depravity, and one knows about *his own* depravity:

> "He also told this parable to some who trusted in themselves that they were righteous and looked down on everyone else: 'Two men went up to the temple to pray, one a Pharisee and the other a tax collector. The Pharisee was standing and praying like this about himself: "God, I thank you that I'm not like other people—greedy, unrighteous, adulterers, or even like this tax collector. I fast twice a week; I give a tenth of everything I get." But the tax collector, standing far off, would not even raise his eyes to heaven but kept striking his chest and saying, "God, have mercy on me, a sinner!" I tell you, this one went down to his house justified rather than the other; because everyone who exalts himself will be humbled, but the one who humbles himself will be exalted.'" (Luke 18 v 9-14)

If Total Depravity reminds us of the depravity of others first, we've become like the Pharisee who prays, *Thank you, God, that I'm not like all these sinners and spiritual losers.* When Total Depravity is something we believe in our hearts, we become the "loser"—the one who prays, "God, have mercy on me, a sinner!"

How often do you think like the Pharisee, patting yourself on the back in view of the problems or personal differences of others? "Thank you, God, that I'm not an Arminian. Praise God that I'm not some fuddy-duddy teetotaler. Father, I'm so glad my marriage and parenting is more honoring to you than you-know-who's. Lord, I just wanna thank you that I'm not some angry atheist who just refuses to see the truth. And, God, thank you that I don't have racist tendencies like Aunt Teetum." A heartfelt understanding of Total Depravity destroys self-righteousness. It will move you to say, even as you notice another's shortcomings and sins, "Oh, God, help me. I'm no better. And I'm helpless without you."

Why did Paul, who ran after holiness harder than all of us, call himself the chief of sinners? Because he was humbled by his depravity and therefore appreciated the grace of God for a sinner like him. "This saying is trustworthy and deserving of full acceptance: 'Christ Jesus came into the world to save sinners'—and I am the worst of them" (1 Timothy 1 v 15).

I am the worst of them. And Christ Jesus still came to save me. That's the heart-cry of a humble Calvinist.

THE DOCTRINE THAT UNDERCUTS RACISM

Total Depravity not only protects us from pride—it protects us from racism. A heart understanding of Total Depravity eradicates any kind of racism in our hearts. No people, tribe, or race outran the curse of sin. Nations and races have committed all kinds of hellish depravity against each other. From the mistreatment of Israelites in Egypt, through the African slave trade, Jim Crow in the United States, Nazi Germany, the Ku Klux Klan, to hate crimes against Syrian refugees in Europe, and right down to sentences said among friends that begin with, "I'm sorry, but Mexicans/Chinese/Italians..."—it all comes from Total Depravity. And once we know Total Depravity, we see that racial superiority is a charade. Every person of every shade of skin under the sun is, by nature, dead in sin. No one is better. Total Depravity explains why racism is so hard to see, repent of, or forgive. Depravity blinds us to depravity.

As John Piper says, "The doctrine of total depravity has a huge role to play in humbling all ethnic groups and giving us a desperate camaraderie of condemnation."[17] We are united in our helplessness, and united in our same source of hope—a risen Israelite, a Middle-Eastern man who is reigning in the heavens.

---

17 John Piper, "The Reformed Faith and Racial Harmony" on the Desiring God blog, https://www.desiringgod.org/messages/the-reformed-faith-and-racial-harmony

DISTANCED FROM THE WORLD

When we misunderstand Total Depravity, we don't only distance ourselves from our own sinfulness. We also distance ourselves from the world.

Jesus said, essentially, that his people are to be in the world but not of the world (John 17 v 11, 16). When we see ourselves as that tax collector in Luke 18 who asked God to be merciful to him did, and not as the Pharisee who's glad he's religious and better, it grows the kind of humility that is determined to pursue holiness but not in a way that retreats in disgust from those around us. If depravity is only or mainly "out there," then I need to retreat, circle the wagons, and protect my family from the world. But since depravity is actually in here, in my heart, I need to repent, and be watchful, as I live in and seek to love this world.

Throughout the Gospels, Jesus is often found with the obviously depraved of society, telling them about the kingdom, offering them hope. Jesus sees the depraved and he doesn't shoo them away, duck and hide, or roll his eyes. He neither excuses their depravity nor distances himself from them because of it. No—Jesus invites himself over for dinner and untangles their depravity. Remember Zacchaeus in Luke 19 v 1-10? When Jesus sees this corrupt government employee sitting on a branch to catch a glimpse of him, he says, *Hey, Zach, come on down, bud. I need to stay at your house today.* While Zacchaeus is ecstatic that Jesus is coming over, the crowds can't fathom why Jesus would want to be around a turncoat, a snake, a sinner, a chief tax collector. After all, Zach's job is to shake down his own people for money to give to Rome. You can see why he's not all that popular. But Jesus doesn't listen to opinion polls.

The unfolding of the story shows why Jesus goes: Zacchaeus repents of his sin. He understands what matters in life, in eternity, in Christ now. And Jesus responds, "[I came] to seek and save the lost" (Luke 19 v 10).

Who are you more prone to think and act like? The crowd grumbling and complaining about sinners, or Jesus, the one drawing near to those in the thick darkness of their depravity? Calvinists can't be the people who refuse to eat with tax collectors and sinners. Let's pick up the tab.

TOTAL SYMPATHY

Arrogance toward fellow sinners, apathy towards people's problems, and cruelty when people confess their sins are all signs that we don't truly know Total Depravity.

A Calvinist should be the most sympathetic person an unbeliever or believer could ever meet. When we see the sinful struggles of our coworkers or family and friends, Total Depravity doesn't teach us to huff and puff in disgust—it warms our heart towards them. We know what it's like to be tripped up and trapped in transgressions. And we know we aren't any better. "Be kind, always showing gentleness to all people. For we too were once foolish, disobedient, deceived, enslaved by various passions and pleasures, living in malice and envy, hateful, detesting one another" (Titus 3 v 2-3). And we are often wooed by these old sins too.

When a brother in Christ, with face in his hands and tears rolling through the gaps in his fingers, confesses his adultery to you, if you know Total Depravity, it shouldn't cause you to flip the table on him—you put your arms around him and his wife. "I love y'all. I'm here." When your sister in Christ admits she's struggling with an eating disorder, you don't respond in disbelief, "Why would you do that to yourself?!" You respond in mercy with a burden-bearing fellowship for your sibling in the Savior. Humility, love, and gentleness flow from knowing our depravity and divine mercy.

The realities and reminders of Total Depravity don't puff us up—they humble us. They make us sympathetic, empathetic, and loving.

TOTAL DEPENDENCY

The first point of Calvinism is about more than how totally depraved we are—it reveals how we are totally dependent on Jesus. We are literally fruitless without him.

In John 15, Jesus shows us the depth our dependence on him: "I am the vine; you are the branches. The one who remains in me and I in him produces much fruit, because you can do nothing without me" (John 15 v 5). You know what we can accomplish without Jesus? Nothing. No righteousness without Jesus. No forgiveness, justification, sanctification, or glorification without Jesus. No "no condemnation" without Jesus. No freedom from sin. No fruit. No fellowship with God. Zip. Zilch. Nada. Jesus is the joyous it-factor of our lives. He makes it happen. So, when I see bushels of the fruit of the Spirit in my life—or even just a few fresh buds—it ain't me. It's Jesus. I got nothing to brag about but him.

The power of God releases us from pride and opens the floodgates of high-powered happiness and joy. "By his power," Paul says, God makes it possible to "fulfill your every desire to do good and your work produced by faith" (2 Thessalonians 1 v 11). Christ lives in us and we live in Christ. Saint Patrick, the fifth-century missionary to Ireland, captured our "in Christ-ness" when he wrote, "Christ with me, Christ before me, Christ behind me, Christ within me, Christ beneath me, Christ above me, Christ at my right, Christ at my left."[18] Our lives are happily dependent on Christ. 24/7/365, and 360 degrees. The Christian life is the life in Christ.

It's no embarrassment to rely on the eternal Son. But pride shames us into believing our power is enough. And as long as I rely on myself for growth, I'll find perpetual frustration and disappointment. I can't grow on my own. I can try to pray for two hours day, read my Bible cover to cover, and be a faithful member of my church, but if Christ isn't at work in me, I'm toast. If I don't rely on Christ, I'm like a lamp unplugged from the outlet. I don't have any

18 Philip Schaff and David Schley Schaff, *History of the Christian Church,* Vol. 4, page 50.

power. I'm not abiding in the power source. We often think Christian maturity is needing help less and less. Wrong. Maturity is realizing how dependent we are on Jesus, more and more. Self-reliance is self-sabotage. But Christ-reliance brings a steady joy in his sanctifying power, knowing that our efforts are backed by his effort. It's no chore for Christ to help his people. He's at work in us, and with Jesus in the driver's seat, we can rejoice, knowing he will bring us home. He's not limited in resources to change us. He will complete his work in us.

THE TOTAL CHRIST

Remember, a Calvinism without Christ is not worth so much as a bouquet of supermarket tulips. So, how does Total Depravity cause us to worship and enjoy the sinless Son of God? By enabling us to be in awe of who he is.

Here is a man who wasn't born totally depraved. From the womb to the tomb, Jesus never committed a sin. No sins of omission—failing to do something he should have done—or sins of commission—doing something he shouldn't have done—could be pinned on him. You sinned while reading this chapter. I'm sure I sinned while writing it. Your day, despite your best and Spirit-assisted efforts, will be marked and marred by sin. You never came under pressure like Jesus did. You never faced the betrayals Jesus did. You never shouldered the burdens Jesus did. But Jesus was tempted in every way that you are, and he never sinned. Not once. Not one ounce of depravity weighed down his thoughts, his words, or his actions, any day, in any way.

Doesn't that leave you marveling at him? Humbled by him?

And consider this: though he never sinned, he was crucified. Depravity happened to Jesus. The eternal, perfect, angel-adored Son of God being stapled to a Roman death-device is the most depraved event in human history. He was a victim of the depraved viciousness of man.

Fleming Rutledge reminds us what the crucified would endure:

"Bodily functions uncontrolled, insects feasting on wounds and orifices, unspeakable thirst, muscle cramps, bolts of pain from the severed median nerves in their wrists, scourged back scraping against the wooden stipes. It is more than any of us are capable of fully imagining. The verbal abuse and other actions such as spitting and throwing refuse by the spectators, Roman soldiers, and passers-by added the final touch."[19]

Rome didn't invent crucifixion, but it perfected it and its messaging:

"It was a form of advertisement, or public announcement—this person is the scum of the earth, not fit to live, more an insect than a human being. The crucified wretch was pinned up like a specimen."[20]

---

19 Fleming Rutledge, *The Crucifixion: Understanding the Death of Jesus Christ*, page 95.

20 *The Crucifixion*, page 92.

Wretch. Jesus experienced the worst of depravity. And he did so to take all of our depravity and sin upon himself. "For our sake [God] made him to be sin who knew no sin, so that in him we might become the righteousness of God" (2 Corinthians 5 v 21, ESV). Here we see the great exchange: Jesus, the infinite and glorious Son of God, took our sin, and we, unworthy and totally depraved sinners, receive his righteousness. Spurgeon unfolds the exchange:

"A spotless Saviour stands in the room [i.e. place] of guilty sinners. God lays upon the spotless Saviour the sin of the guilty, so that he becomes, in the expressive language of the text, sin. Then he takes off from the innocent Saviour his righteousness, and puts that to the account of the once-guilty sinners, so that the sinners become righteousness—righteousness of the highest and divinest source—the righteousness of God in Christ Jesus."[21]

Jesus came for the depraved—he stood in our shoes, drowned in the dregs of our depravity, and gave us his life. "For I came not to call the righteous, but sinners" (Matthew 9 v 13). I'm so glad he came for sinners, because this means I qualify. You do too.

John Newton, the former slave-trader and no stranger to the depravity of humanity, understood grace. In that most famous of hymns, *Amazing Grace*, Newton writes

---

21 C.H. Spurgeon, "Christ Made Sin," in *The Metropolitan Tabernacle Pulpit Sermons*, pages 301-302.

with humble self-awareness: God rescued "a wretch like me." Not a wretch like them. Not a wretch like those unbelievers, or those less mature Christians, or those believers who have really messed up. A wretch *like me*. That's heart-knowledge of Total Depravity. And knowing he was a wretch meant Newton could appreciate the magnificence of God's mercy. Total depravity, when we apply it first and foremost to ourselves, lowers us to the foot of the cross, to where we can look up at the glory of grace. Grace becomes amazing when we behold it as self-confessed wretches—when we can sing and mean that he saved a wretch like *me*.

Jesus came to redeem people who could never measure up. We can trick Disney but we can't sneak past God. We could stand on our tippy toes, straining to meet his standards of righteousness, but it would never work. We are—infinitely and eternally—so far short. But in Christ, we not only measure up—we are now co-heirs of the Almighty's amusement park, the universe. We own it. All that is Christ's is ours. Real Calvinism is a humble and happy enjoyment of God's grace for sinners like us. Amazing grace, that saved a wretch like... me.

4. THE PREQUEL TO YOUR FAITH

Prequels can cause problems. Whether we are talking about the *Lord of the Rings* films and the later-released prequel, *The Hobbit* (and yes, I know they were books way before they were films), or the prequels in the *Star Wars* saga featuring the most unloveable character in movie history (Jar Jar Binks), tempers flare and eye-rolling begins. Some people care way too much about the place of prequels and others don't care at all.

But I love a *good* prequel. Who doesn't love the "aha!" moments they provide? Background information found in prequels heightens and deepens the stories we know and love. Character arcs, plot development, insights, and connected dots provided by prequels make the stories we enjoy even sweeter.

And there is one prequel every Christian can enjoy. Predestination is the prequel to your faith in Christ.

YOU'RE ON THE ROSTER

The second point in the doctrines of grace answers the question that naturally follows from the truth of Total Depravity. Why in the world does anyone get saved if we are so warped in our nature and will, and unable to turn to God? Unconditional Election is the explanation.

If you believe in Christ, it's because God decided to save you long before you saw you needed to be saved. Before you were born, God already loved you. When your heart first swelled with joy over the forgiveness you found in the crucified and risen Christ, you didn't sway God to let you into his kingdom—your name was already on the roster.

Paul writes an extended flow of praise of God's grace in Ephesians 1, and here we find an exposition of God's sovereign grace for sinners.

"For he chose us in him, before the foundation of the world, to be holy and blameless in love before him. He predestined us to be adopted as sons through Jesus Christ for himself, according to the good pleasure of his will, to the praise of his glorious grace that he lavished on us in the Beloved One."

(Ephesians 1 v 4-6)

Election means that before the events of Genesis 1 v 1 unfolded in space and in time, the triune God chose which depraved sinners would receive his mercy in Jesus Christ. God chose who would be saved.

In his God-given glimpse of heavenly reality, the apostle John saw the Lamb's book of life—written before earth's crust was established. This book contains the names of everyone who will be redeemed by the blood of Christ (Revelation 13 v 8; 21 v 27). In heaven, right now, there is a page in the Lamb's book of life with "Jeffrey Alan Medders" on it. For a moment, think about your name and about that book. If you are in Christ, your name is there too. And your name is written in ink older than the dirt in Jerusalem. What grace!

Christian, arrangements were made for you long before you took your first breath, committed your first sin, and sang your first hymn. God knew you would come to faith. God set your destination long before you could crawl. He predestined you to be adopted into his family by the death and resurrection of the Son of God. He wasn't surprised when faith flamed in your heart. He knew the day was coming. He planned it.

And God's plan to save particular sinners for eternity was, and is, unconditional. No human factors were considered in God's election. No conditions outside of God played a role in his choosing. Election was all, as Paul says, "according to the good pleasure of his will." Spurgeon, as usual, hit the high note on this when he said:

"I believe the doctrine of election, because I am quite sure that if God had not chosen me I should never have chosen him; and I am sure he chose me before I was born, or else he never would have chosen me afterwards; and he must have elected me for reasons unknown to me, for I never could find any reason in myself why he should have looked upon me with special love."[22]

God didn't look at the schoolyard of humanity and pick out the best, brightest, and most gifted and talented he could find to play on his team. There were no best. We were all dull and dark in our hearts. "No other cause," Calvin says, "makes us God's children but only his choice of us in himself."[23] God made his choice according to his mysterious, merciful will, to the praise of his glorious grace.

CORRIDOR OF TIME, CRYSTAL BALL, OR CHOICE?

In an effort to unravel this mystery of mercy, folks will explain predestination and God's foreknowledge as God choosing those whom he knew would choose him. Did God look down the corridors of time and base his election on who would respond to the gospel? That's not the testimony of the Scriptures. God consulting with the future sounds like he polished off a crystal ball, an amulet, or some magical housewares to see if he could learn something he didn't already know. "Mirror, mirror, on the wall, show me who will respond to the gospel call." Didn't happen. Paul tells us in Romans 8 about the domino effect of sovereign grace:

"We know that all things work together for the good of those who love God, who are called according to his

22 C.H. Spurgeon, *The Sword and Trowel*, page 38.

23 John Calvin, *Sermon on Ephesians*, page 39.

purpose. For those he foreknew he also predestined to be conformed to the image of his Son, so that he would be the firstborn among many brothers and sisters. And those he predestined, he also called; and those he called, he also justified; and those he justified, he also glorified." (Romans 8 v 28-30)

God's foreknowing in predestination was a foreknowing of those people. Paul isn't telling us about the things God knew in advance, but rather the things he planned irrevocably in advance. He's telling us about the biography of believers, the "those"—those who love God, those who are called because of God's purpose, those whom God foreknew, predestined, called, justified, and glorified. As John Piper says, "Faith is not a condition for election. Just the reverse. Election is a condition for faith."[24]

So, do we choose God, or does God choose us? Yes. Our choosing of Christ and God's choosing for us are not running in different directions. Spurgeon was asked to reconcile these two truths as they are expressed by Jesus in the Gospel of John: "Everyone the Father gives me will come to me, and the one who comes to me I will never cast out" (John 6 v 37). Here we see the Father giving people to his Son, and people coming to his Son—God's choice and human choice, in one sentence. How, Spurgeon was asked, do you reconcile these two truths? His answer? "I never

---

24 John Piper, *Five Points: Towards a Deeper Experience of God's Grace*, page 53.

reconcile friends."[25] Election doesn't erase our choosing of Christ. You really did choose him. Election shows the chronology of choice. God chose you *before* you chose him. You freely chose to put your faith in God because God had freely chosen to bring you to faith. We chose second because God chose first.

Yes, election is a mystery we can't fully get our heads around from our time-limited, creaturely perspective— but ultimately there's no reconciliation needed. And when we see what fruit grows in the soil of this gracious doctrine, we get less consumed with arguing over it because we are too busy enjoying it. Let's be too happy in his sovereignty and too busy rejoicing to get mad about it.

STABILIZED IN SOVEREIGN LOVE

Imagine if God's choosing to save me was conditional. I'd become a seriously unstable person. Doubt and fear would live in my mind. How can I be sure that I checked the right boxes? What if he decides to release me because I'm not meeting his conditions? And on the other side of the road, if God did choose me because of me, I'd be so full of myself that elevators wouldn't be able support the weight of my pride. If something we did got us in with God, then we aren't freely loved by God—we earned his love by wisely putting our faith in him or by diligently doing good works for him, and we may somehow lose his love again. Conditional love makes us anxious, defensive,

25 C.H. Spurgeon, "High Doctrine and Broad Doctrine," in *The Metropolitan Tabernacle Pulpit Sermons,* Vol. 30, page 49.

self-justifying. That's no way to live, not only because it's miserable but because it's not true.

God doesn't love us because we chose him. He chose us because he loves us. As J.B. Phillips translates Ephesians 1 v 4-5, "He planned, *in his purpose of love*, that we should be adopted as his own children through Jesus Christ—that we might learn to praise that glorious generosity of his which has made us welcome *in the everlasting love* he bears towards the Son" (my italics). Love was his purpose. He chose because he loves with an everlasting love, and he elected to bring us into his eternal love. We are stabilized in his love.

Knowing unconditional election doesn't puff up our chests—it takes the breath out of them. "In him we have also received an inheritance, because we were predestined according to the plan of the one who works out everything in agreement with the purpose of his will" (Ephesians 1 v 11). When you realize the mega-magnitude of this truth, you are left in awe of sovereign grace.

No one has ever loved you like God does.

Election means God loved you before anyone else did. Way before. The almighty God was the first person to ever love you. God made plans to take care of you, eternally, when you didn't ask him to. God decided to give you an inheritance with the Son without getting second opinions or calling your references.

Why did God show you this mercy? Because he wanted to. "For he tells Moses, 'I will show mercy to whom I will show mercy, and I will have compassion on whom I will have compassion'" (Romans 9 v 15). God's mercy comes with a hue of mystery. Why me? Why you? Why anyone?! Because God, of his own free will, displayed his mercy, compassion, grace, and love. So now I'm neither puffed up by success nor crushed by failure. I'm loved, regardless. Stability and humility are found in God's sovereign grace.

HUMBLED TO LOVE ONE ANOTHER

Unconditional election shows us the way we are to love one another. We're to love unconditionally:

"Love consists in this: not that we loved God, but that he loved us and sent his Son to be the atoning sacrifice for our sins. Dear friends, if God loved us in this way, we also must love one another."

(1 John 4 v 10-11)

Here's John's logic. Love is God loving us. Love is God loving us without us doing anything to deserve it. Now, if you know God loved you like that, you go love others the same. The way of God's love is the way we love others. It's unconditional. It's about us choosing to love, regardless of what comes back.

I've yet to find a command in the New Testament that says, *Love one another, as long the person is loveable, deserves it, and agrees with you*. It doesn't exist. Grace rebuilds what it means to love. Heart-Calvinism teaches us to love one another without condition.

Election isn't confined to pages in our Bibles and books. It's 3D. It hugs you and shakes your hand on Sundays. Maybe it helps you move from your third-floor apartment. You see election while sitting in a small group filled with varying ages, races, and backgrounds. It's easy to learn about a doctrine in a book, but you live and love in the midst of sovereign grace. Every Christian you see, you are seeing election.

At the end of Paul's letter to the Romans, he tells the church in Rome, "Greet Rufus, chosen in the Lord" (Romans 16 v 13). Paul takes an action of God from eternity past and says that is the lens through which Rufus should be viewed in the present. He is a ripened fruit of sovereign grace. He is a chosen one. Paul wants the Christians in Rome to look at Rufus and think, "My elect brother." Rufus is a grand recipient of supernatural grace—and so is every Christian you meet.

Don't think here of the brothers and sisters in Christ you naturally "click" with—the ones whom it takes almost no effort to get along with, to love, and to experience real Christian community with. Think of the brothers or sisters you struggle to be around. You know God loves them, but you'd honestly rather get a cavity filled—without novocaine—than fill your calendar with them. Your heart sinks when you're drawn into conversation with them or when they move into your small group.

Now, instead of seeing those as people who don't quite meet your conditions of acceptance, see them as chosen in the Lord. That brother who can't help but make every conversation he has with you an awkward one—you are talking to one loved from eternity by the Ancient of Days. He matters to God. He should matter to you. That sister in Christ who is always trying to wiggle her way into a conversation she's not a part of, who texts too much, and who doesn't know boundaries—don't define her as a nuisance. She is a royal heir of the kingdom, chosen in the Lord. God loves her. How can you not? Every Christian you meet is a manifestation of predestination, of God's unconditional decision to love those who don't deserve it. "If God loved us in this way, we also must love one another."

When we've been humbled by the sovereign love of God, we grow in humility toward one another. We Calvinists are passionate about Romans 9 v 16: "So then, it does not depend on human will or effort but on God who shows mercy." And we should be just as passionate about Romans 12 v 16: "Live in harmony with one another. Do not be proud; instead, associate with the humble. Do not be wise in your own estimation." The exhortation to live in harmony is here because there is an ever-present temptation to fall into discord. While differences among Christians are unavoidable, division can be avoided. Personality differences, personal preferences and opinions, political and theological differences, and cultural and ethnic diversity are all opportunities for the unconditional grace of God to harmonize the people of God. We don't lose our differences; we just refuse to make others lose out to them. We sing the same song in different harmonies: "Blessing and honor and glory and power be to the one seated on the throne, and to the Lamb, forever and ever!" (Revelation 5 v 13). The Lamb unites us in his holy glory.

At our church, our elders are unashamed about the doctrines of grace. They're in our doctrinal statement and distinctives. I teach our view of election in the membership class, but we don't make someone's membership contingent on their view of election. We have Arminian-leaning members, we have Calvinist-leaning members— and we have confused or unsure members too. But I can't remember the last time we had a debate or fight over election. You know why? Because Jesus is first. He unites us together. We show grace to one another and love one another the way Christ has loved us. We commit to not being divisive, argumentative, or arrogant about our doctrine. Everyone is treated with dignity. Every believer you meet is a part of the royal, royally chosen, family.

DESTINATION HOLINESS

The doctrine of election wants to take us somewhere more important than a Bible boxing ring. Calvin reminds us, "But ye must always bear in mind that God's electing of us was in order to call us to holiness of life."[26] Holiness is the destination of predestination. "For he chose us in him, before the foundation of the world, *to be holy and*

---

26 John Calvin, *Sermons on Ephesians*, page 36.

blameless..." (Ephesians 1 v 4, my italics). Holiness is where we are headed. We were predestined to be molded into the image, character, and way of Christ (Romans 8 v 29). Far from leading us toward arrogance, election humbles us toward holiness, and God's sovereign love is the locomotive power to get us there.

When news of God's sovereign love first landed in my ears, an earthquake hit my heart. Predestination rattled me, in a good way. As a sophomore in high school, a speck among 800 other sophomores, I was as uncool as sociologically possible. I never went to a dance, I never went on a date, I was too short to make it on the basketball team, and my skin and hairstyle refused to cooperate with my plans to not be lame. All I had going for me was a starting spot in the puppet ministry at my church. Puppets, y'all. High school was rough.

But my lack of coolness isn't what made these years so crushing. My hidden sin and hypocrisy did. I led Bible studies and played my acoustic guitar in the youth band all while I was enslaved to pornography. I didn't know what to do, who to talk to, or how to stop. The shame shackled me. I knew my parents would flip. My Christian friends and I didn't talk about the matters of the heart and soul—we debated theology and played video games instead. All of this added up to a profound amount of insecurity. Loser, hypocrite, disgusting.

But one Sunday, as the preacher walked us through Ephesians 1 v 3-14, I perked up. Instead of using my Bible to turn my arm into the perfect kickstand for my head for the weekly nap, I was tracking with the passage—verse by verse, word by word. An internal dialogue began in that pink-cushioned church pew, and it lasted for days.

"God predestined me to be saved? *Me?*"

"Yes."

"So, the one who spoke nebulae and galaxies into existence and is robed in unapproachable light? *He* chose me?"

"That's what Paul said."

"Okay. Hold on. The only true God, the one surrounded by angels swirling and singing, 'Holy, Holy, Holy!'? He loved me before he gave earth its shape?"

"You are reading it right."

"Loser me? Hypocrite me? Porn-addicted me? The Almighty not only wanted to save this mess but found joy in me? *Why?* Why would God care about me? I'm nothing, nobody."

And then the earthquake.

God's love shook the lukewarmness out of my heart. Sovereign love set me upright. Insecurities and sophomoric ways were pushed out by the expulsive power of this new affection: God. God is love. As the old song goes, "Love lifted me!"—it lifted me toward holiness.

Predestination conquered my craving for pornography. Instead of cycling through images in my mind when trying to fall asleep, I was thinking about election and God's love. I saw my sin and the great love of God, and my sin became bitter next to the deep richness of sovereign grace.

The doctrine of election is often found at the heart of heated debates. But it was designed to be found in the heat of battle. The precious truth of election is a serrated point on the double-edged sword of the Spirit. It tells us of God's love for his children: a love we did not earn and cannot lose. It slays dragons. It soothes saints. It makes principalities and powers flee. It cuts temptation down to size. It detaches idols. It changes us.

When the love of God gripped my heart, my heart let go of the clods of mud I thought were so precious. I could hear a holiday at the beach being offered to me. My love for God grew, weakening my love for this sin, as I saw his love for me: "We love because he first loved us" (1 John 4 v 19).

It wasn't predestination, per se, that severed my craving for digitized hook-ups—it was the love of Jesus displayed in predestination. Even more, it was (and is) Jesus himself. Jesus is the expulsive power in our affections. Jesus is more exciting, invigorating, and satisfying than anything that moth, rust, or high-speed internet could destroy.

God's love is leading us into the likeness of the Son. What are the sins you are struggling to stay away from? What are the cravings of your flesh? What is luring you from the path of faithfulness to your risen Lord? Look it full in the face and tell it, "I'm not chosen for you. You don't love me. You are not there for me, unconditionally. I belong to Christ. I'm being made like Christ." Turn. Walk in God's love. You were elected for this transformation.

PREDESTINATION AND THE PRIDE PROBLEM

A head-only grip on unconditional election makes pride and predestination into frenemies. We know pride is a sinister enemy of Christians, but when it comes to disagreements over the doctrines of grace, somehow we welcome pride in as our friend and ally. We need to end our friendship with pride. Frenemies no more.

I'll never forget what a fifty-something-year-old mom asked me while riding in the busted-up church van for a youth trip.

"What should we think about people who refuse to believe in election?"

I was puzzled.

"What do you mean?" I asked.

"I mean..." She paused and leaned in. "Are they even saved?"

My response? "Well, have you always understood election the way you do now?"

She furrowed her brow. "Well, no, I guess not."

"Well, ma'am, were you a believer before you believed this way?"

Brow unfurrowed. A series of nods commenced.

"I see what you are saying, but..."

I could've felt proud as we spoke—I believed in election like her, and I wasn't being judgmental like her. And I would have felt that way too—if the Spirit hadn't tapped me on the shoulder: *Hey, you realize you've often been on the other side of this conversation? The judgmental one?* Many times before, I had thought the same things: "Are they even saved—those people who say they trust Christ but don't agree with election?" And I know brothers and sisters who, even as they've grappled with the doctrine of unconditional election, have been told, "If you think about this, and then reject it, you are rejecting the authority of the Scriptures, and so you are rejecting Christ." This is something we Calvinists must continually be cautious of—because we are adding to what it means to be saved by Jesus, and that's as un-Calvinistic and, more importantly, un-Christian as it gets. When you question the salvation of an Arminian (or anyone else) because they aren't a Calvinist, you are adding to faith alone in Christ alone. It's a denial of the Reformation's battle cry: *Christ alone.*

Understanding election in the exact way we Calvinists do isn't what makes or breaks someone's Christianity. Faith in the crucified and risen Jesus for their sins is *it*. No asterisks. No "I-see-what-you-are-saying-buts." If we add any of our precious views—even the doctrines of grace— we end up betraying grace.

Don't think you'd never do such a thing. It can happen to the maturest of believers. We know that because it happened to an apostle. In Galatians 2, we hear about Peter walking away from a table of Gentiles. Peter used to eat with them, fellowshipping with them and enjoying their company. But when a certain group of legalistic Jews came to town, Peter moved the goalposts and his dinner plate. He added conditions to his love and fellowship. He decided he shouldn't, couldn't, wouldn't have meaningful fellowship with uncircumcised Christians. Peter believed that kosher-keeping Sabbatarians were now the line of acceptable fellowship for him. You can hear Peter say, *I can only fellowship with like-minded believers.*

Paul saw this and decided he must give Peter a piece of his mind—or rather, give him the gospel. He confronted Peter in front of everyone because, "I saw that they were deviating from the truth of the gospel" (Galatians 2 v 14). Peter and those he influenced detoured from radical grace into legalism. He didn't deny the cross and resurrection of Jesus—but he added to it, and so he diluted it. Peter's actions preached a gospel-denying hypocrisy that said that Jesus is enough to save us, but he's not enough to unify us. Christ alone saves, but we need more conditions if we are going to have fellowship. Peter didn't walk in love. He actually walked away—literally and theologically.

How many times have we done this? Have we ever made Calvinism, instead of Christ, the comfortable terms of Christian love and fellowship? Whether we do it explicitly or implicitly, either breaking fellowship or never giving fellowship a chance because of the way someone views election, we "love" with conditions—and that is a betrayal of unconditional election.

IN CHRIST, TO CHRIST, FOR CHRIST

How do we get the doctrine of election in our hearts? Well, when we think about the doctrine of election, we typically think of the what, when, why, how—and we forget to glory in the supreme *who*: Christ. Election isn't a bland, aimless, or monotone theological category. It's the multi-sensory glory of Christ dazzling in high definition with a symphony of savory joys. Predestination works because of the work of Christ—his death for our sins and his supernatural resurrection from the dead. We are chosen *in* and *for* the Chosen One. We were predestined to be united to the Son of God forever. Election is about us saints, but not chiefly. Election is supremely about Christ, the one who has first place in everything (Colossians 1 v 18).

God's sovereign grace is lavished on us in the Beloved One (Ephesians 1 v 6). Every blessing we enjoy is because of Christ—his accomplishments and his being the risen Son of God. The new "in-Christ-ness" we have is what defines us. Every fruit we bear, every we sin repent of, and every comfort we feel is all because of the Messiah. Paul tells us that "every one of God's promises is 'Yes' in him" (2 Corinthians 1 v 20). The promises of God, whether in the Old or New Testament, are answered, fulfilled, and kept because of Jesus. He's *the* Chosen One, through whom God gathers his chosen ones. And because of God's mercy, we reap a harvest of blessings in our election for connection to the Beloved Son. We are:

- crucified with Christ (Galatians 2 v 20)

- buried with Christ (Colossians 2 v 12)

- raised with Christ in his resurrection (Romans 6 v 5)

- seated with Christ in the heavens (Ephesians 2 v 6)

- forgiven in Christ (Ephesians 4 v 32)

- justified, declared righteous in Christ (Romans 8 v 1)

- made new creations in Christ (2 Corinthians 5 v 17)

- sanctified in Christ (1 Corinthians 1 v 2)

- joined to the church in Christ (Galatians 3 v 28)

- called coheirs of the kingdom in Christ (Ephesians 3 v 6)

It's all because of Christ. We were chosen to belong to Jesus. We were elected to exalt the risen King.

Predestination is the backstory of your faith in Christ. Ephesians 1 reminds us of God's end goal of election: the praise of his grace. As far as I can tell, God didn't elect us to go punch holes in the theology of our brothers and sisters.

The truth of election is meant to move you to praise the One who loved you before the foundation of the world, and who will love you 10 billion years (and counting) from now. Let this grace cause you to worship him with more than just your mind. Engage your heart. A sign of heart-Calvinism is that we don't get our jollys in arguing about election, and we don't feel that we have to question the salvation of those who don't hold to our view. Rather, grace in the heart means we become more humble, and more holy, and more loving. Unconditionally.

5. THE CROSS, THE CHURCH, AND THE COSMOS

My wife loves chocolate—and she's got expensive tastebuds. Natalie craves the dark stuff. She's not interested in a bar of chocolate made in Pennsylvania, trucked to Texas, and parked on a shelf for weeks. The fresh cacao is what she likes. And we must be blessed and highly favored because we live a mile and a half from the first bean-to-bar chocolate-makers in Texas. Fresh, dark, $7.00 chocolate bars are just a short drive away.

When I come home with a spread of chocolate bars and a box of fresh truffles, my daughter's eyes expand as she squeals, "Yum! Are those for me?" Uhh, no. You can have the cheap stuff. These are for my wife. And for my wife only. My gift has an intentional recipient. I had Natalie in mind as I picked out the bars and truffles, stood in line, handed over my debit card, and ignored whatever the total was on the receipt. I smiled as I got into my truck and imagined Natalie's smile when she saw what I'd bought for her.

My gift was for a particular person, deliberately and lovingly bought for her, and deliberately and lovingly given to her.

It's a strange link from my wife's love of dark chocolate to our Lord's atoning death on the cross, but in a sense we're talking about the same thing—a deliberately bought gift, with intentional recipients. When we discuss the extent of the atonement, we are talking about the intentions of the Atoner.

While Unconditional Election is the petal in TULIP debated among most Christians, Limited Atonement is the subject of intra-tribal debate among Calvinists. "Four-Point Calvinists" exist in this space. Even among the "Young, Restless, and Reformed" crowd, Limited Atonement has limited acceptance. It's the least popular point in the set. Why is that?

LET'S STOP LIMITING

Limited Atonement doesn't sit well with a lot of people because of the way it's taught and talked about. It's negative from the start. A cold, non-nuanced statement majoring on who Jesus didn't die for doesn't quite stir the affections. It's also not in tune with the tone of Scripture. The gospel of grace isn't the announcement of what Jesus didn't do. *Hear ye! Hear ye! Jesus did not die for thee—maybe.* No one wants to hear that. And they shouldn't. We should speak of what Jesus did, what he accomplished, and what he offers to sinners.

Starting the conversation on the atonement with a negative posture is going to bring about a negative result. I've been in these conversations. I've been the negative new Calvinist, thinking I'm going to liberate people from their poor theology with an argument for a limited atonement. Guess how many people I convinced. It's the same number of broccoli florets I ate last year—zero. But guess how many heated conversations I ignited. It's the same number of tortilla chips I ate last month—too many to track. So, we need to reframe the point. Let's bring a sweet aroma to this petal by back-pedaling for a moment.

We misunderstand the atonement if we argue over the extent of it more than we want to exclaim about the fact that Jesus died for sinners at all. We ought to be floored by the truth of God the Son dying for anyone. Even before crossing our Ts with the extent of the atonement, we ought to stop in our tracks and be in awe of it all. Let's marvel that Jesus humbled himself to levels the world has never seen, all so he could save humans like us. He's so kind and merciful to us merciless people.

DEFINED DEFINITELY

Like most people who write and speak on TULIP, I also want to lobby for not using the word "limited" as the headline for this point. Phrases like "particular redemption," or my favorite, "definite atonement," far better represent the point being made, though I know it puts the acronym in jeopardy (TUDIP, anyone?) A "limited" atonement can make it sound like Jesus' death on the cross didn't pack enough power needed to redeem all of us from our sins, as though his death was missing something. No, Jesus' death is not limited in its potency, sufficiency, or design. The sonic boom of our Savior's death is bigger, not smaller, than the paths our minds travel along when we hear "limited." We'll ride the wave to new terrain by the end of this chapter. Hang in there.

But before we define definite atonement and limit ourselves from using the word "limited," there is a point to make about that word "limited." It's this: almost everyone "limits" the atonement in one way or another. Unless you're a universalist, who thinks that Christ's death saves everyone regardless of their response to the gospel, you limit, or define, the atonement's effects. All orthodox Christians "limit" the atonement as being effective for those who have placed their faith in Christ's death in their place.

The Calvinist doctrine of Limited Atonement limits the scope of the atonement while expressing its effectiveness—Jesus' death redeemed his people, specifically, from sin. Holding to a position that rejects Limited Atonement on the one hand and universalism on the other means you expand the scope of the atonement while limiting its effectiveness—Jesus' death made redemption possible for all people. You either limit its application or its achievement. Did Jesus atone, or did he make atonement attainable? Has salvation been purchased, or has it only been made possible?

Definite Atonement teaches that Jesus didn't only clear a path out of the burning building and tell us to run: *Look, I made a way. Go!* No—it says that he is the way. As the walls crumbled he picked up our comatose bodies and, his hair singed by the flames, he revived us and threw us out the window—and then the building of God's wrath and justice against our sin collapsed on him. His death redeemed— done, past tense—us from the curse of the law (Galatians 3 v 13). John Murray sums it up this way: "Christ did not come to put men in a redeemable position but to redeem himself a people."[27]

The blood-splattered pulpit-cross, where the Lord Jesus announced, "It is finished!" achieved exactly what it was designed to do. Jesus purchased people for God with his blood from every tribe and language and people and nation (Revelation 5 v 9). Design-specs fulfilled. David Gibson and Jonathan Gibson connect the term "definite atonement" to a perhaps surprising word—"beautiful":

"Definite atonement is beautiful because it tells the story of the Warrior-Son who comes to earth to slay his enemy and rescue his Father's people. He is the

---

27 John Murray, *Redemption Accomplished and Applied*, page 63.

Good Shepherd who lays down his life for the sheep, a loving Bridegroom who gives himself for his bride, and a victorious King who lavishes the spoils of his conquest on the citizens of his realm."[28]

Defining the atonement as a Definite Atonement is far better than as a Limited Atonement. It puts the focus back on what Jesus did, not on what he didn't do. When Jesus died on that criminal's cross, he took the sins of his people, he paid for them, and he gives his people—his sheep, his bride, his church—his righteousness (2 Corinthians 5 v 21). Definite Atonement means that Jesus' death definitely and explicitly, surely and indubitably, absolutely and incontestably paid for the sins of all who would believe in him.

A DEFINED DESIGN

Definite Atonement—the death of the Lamb of God—is the next logical domino from Unconditional Election. The Lamb was slain for the people listed in the Lamb's book of life. The Son died on the cross specifically for those the Father had chosen before the creation specifically. But I don't think you should believe in Definite Atonement simply because it's the logical outworking of predestination. Don't believe something simply because it makes sense. You should believe it if you see it in the Scriptures. Don't take a Calvinist's word for it.

---

28 Ed. Jonathan and David Gibson, *From Heaven He Came and Sought Her: Definite Atonement in Historical, Biblical, Theological, and Pastoral Perspective*, page 17.

Matthew tells us, right at the start of his Gospel, who Jesus came to save from their sins. An angel of the Lord surprises Joseph, and tells him that his betrothed is pregnant by the Holy Spirit, and that...

> "she will give birth to a son, and you are to name him Jesus, because he will save *his people* from their sins." (Matthew 1 v 21, my italics)

The "his" makes the difference. Even Jesus' very name has a definite design to it. God saves.

During his public ministry, Jesus clarified who he is and who he was going to the cross for:

> "I am the good shepherd. I know my own, and my own know me, just as the Father knows me, and I know the Father. I lay down my life *for the sheep*. But I have other sheep that are not from this sheep pen; I must bring them also, and they will listen to my voice. Then there will be one flock, one shepherd."
>
> (John 10 v 14-16, my italics)

Jesus doesn't see *everyone* as his own. He's got his own people, as we saw in Matthew, and they are *the sheep*. There's a clear sense that Jesus knew precisely who he was going to be dying for. Jesus died on that splintery cross for the sheep. And not just the sheep in Israel, but sheep spread across history and geography. Sheep like me—half-Mexican, full-Texan. Sheep who, if you believe in Jesus, are not merely *like* you, but actually, definitely *you*.

JESUS DID DIE FOR ALL

Jesus died for his people—and yet the Bible is also clear that, yes, he died for all people. "For there is one God and one mediator between God and humanity, the man Christ Jesus, who gave himself as a ransom for all, a testimony at the proper time" (1 Timothy 2 v 5-6). Calvin himself says this is a universal "all":

"The universal term all must always be referred to classes of men, and not to persons; as if he had said, that not only Jews, but Gentiles also, not only persons of humble rank, but princes also, were redeemed by the death of Christ. Since, therefore, he wishes the benefit of his death to be common to all, an insult is offered to him by those who, by their opinion, shut out any person from the hope of salvation."[29]

But notice what Calvin is and isn't saying. He's arguing that when the Scripture says that Jesus died for all, it means he died for *all kinds of people*. Before you roll your eyes, I know this looks like a sleight-of-hand cop-out from the controversy. It's not. It's actually lining up with the controversy of the New Testament.

A chronic battle in the early church was the Jew-and-Gentile/Greek tension. After years—centuries—of division, Christ brought them together, and they had a hard time gelling. But the truth is that, "there is no

---

29 John Calvin and William Pringle, *Commentaries on the Epistles to Timothy, Titus, and Philemon*, page 57.

distinction between Jew and Greek, because the same Lord of all richly blesses all who call on him" (Romans 10 v 12). The Lord of all, Jews and Greeks, blesses all who call on him. All kinds of sinners, not just Jews. Jesus made atonement for all kinds of sinners, without distinction. Paul goes out of his way to stress this truth: Jesus died to save Jews, Greeks, women, men, rich, poor, slave, free:

- "Yet to those who are called, *both Jews and Greeks*, Christ is the power of God and the wisdom of God" (1 Corinthians 1 v 24, my italics).

- "For we were all baptized by one Spirit into one body—*whether Jews or Greeks, whether slaves or free*—and we were all given one Spirit to drink" (1 Corinthians 12 v 13, my italics).

- "There is no *Jew or Greek, slave or free, male and female*; since you are all one in Christ Jesus" (Galatians 3 v 28, you know who's putting in the italics by now).

- "In Christ there is not *Greek and Jew, circumcision and uncircumcision, barbarian, Scythian, slave and free*; but Christ is all and in all" (Colossians 3 v 11).

Jonathan Gibson helps us here:

"The reason that at times Paul employs universalistic language in relation to the atonement is because he is confronting a heresy in the church that promoted salvation for an elite and exclusive few. Paul is emphatic in such contexts: Christ died for all, for the world, for Jew and Gentile ... In this regard the 'all without distinction' meaning should be seen for what it actually is: all-inclusive, all-embracing—no one is left out: not Gentile, not women, not slave, not barbarian, not children, not elderly, not poor, not white, not black—not anyone!"[30]

When the apostle John says Jesus atoned for the sins of the world, he is pressing the same truth as Paul. "He himself is the atoning sacrifice for our sins, and not only for ours, but also for those of the whole world" (1 John 2 v 2). He died for the world—the word means world. But we have a dilemma.

Five-Point Calvinists are often charged with saying that world doesn't mean world. But in reality, unless you are a universalist, we all wrestle with how we should understand Jesus' death for the world. If you take 1 John 2 v 2 without any theological interpretation, you'd think Jesus already saved every single person in the world. But we know from the rest of Scripture that that's not what John means. Even in 1 John, the apostle makes a clear distinction between "God's children and the devil's children"—and it is "everyone who believes that Jesus is the Christ [who] has been born of God" (3 v 10; 5 v 1). His gospel is clear: "to all *who did receive him*, he gave them the right to be children of God, to *those who believe in his name*" (John 1 v 12,

<hr>

30 *From Heaven He Came and Sought Her*, page 330.

my italics). Unless we're to ignore the rest of Scripture, we have to nuance how John is using "world."

Jesus is the Savior of the world—of anyone, anywhere, who receives him—and Jesus is the Savior of the world— defined as the elect sheep from all over the world, who will receive him. Anyone in the world, from Mozambique to Manhattan, can be saved by Jesus. John, just like Paul, is showing that Jesus is not a regional or race-based Savior. The only Savior for this world is Jesus. His death is sufficient. There is a Savior for people beyond Israel and the surrounding Mediterranean people, because Jesus is a worldwide Savior. This is shown when John amplifies the words of the high priest shortly before Jesus' death: "He prophesied that Jesus was going to die for the nation, and not for the nation only, but also to unite the scattered children of God" (John 11 v 51-52). Jesus has sheep not just in the pen of Israel but scattered abroad in every tribe, language, and people group. He is the Savior of the world, without saving everyone in the world.

JESUS' DEATH AND THE COSMOS

There is one more dimension to Jesus' death for the world, and we almost never talk about it.

"World" in the New Testament also means more than a collection of people. It often means more than our world. It's the cosmos. In examining the extent of the atonement, we can all—whether we accept definite atonement or not— accidentally undersell the magnitude of Jesus' death.

The *universe* benefits from the work of the Lord Jesus.

There is a sense in which Jesus died for clownfish. Jesus' death affects Mount Everest. There are stars, quasars, and galaxies that receive blessings because of the death of the Son of Man. He didn't atone for the sins of the soil beneath your feet—but he did die to release the soil from the burden, decay, and groaning caused by the sin of those who tread on it. Jesus' death and resurrection is the guarantee that he is going to renovate the universe when he returns. "Then the one seated on the throne said, 'Look, I am making everything new'" (Revelation 21 v 5).

Jesus is, in a sense, redeeming pineapples, bonsai trees, and even broccoli. Jesus' victory over sin means the universe doesn't have to be tossed into a divine garbage can. Since Jesus defeated the grave, the entire creation is leaning forward, groaning and waiting for when God's children will be made new, because it is next:

> "For the creation eagerly waits with anticipation for God's sons to be revealed. For the creation was subjected to futility—not willingly, but because of him who subjected it—in the hope that the creation itself will also be set free from the bondage to decay into the glorious freedom of God's children. For we know that the whole creation has been groaning together with labor pains until now." (Romans 8 v 19-22)

Christ's death is supercharged to remake the heavens and the earth. His death is more powerful than we realize.

Christ's cross released Saturn and its rings from decay, just as it set us free from our sins. His atonement is far more powerful and far more wide-ranging than any of us tend to realize or can really ever grasp.

THE ATONEMENT DEFINITELY HUMBLES US

Stop and think for a moment about how the atonement defines you and me.

I was born a transgressor. A cosmic criminal. I definitely broke God's law. I am guilty as charged before the Almighty. That's who I am. Or rather, that's who I was.

But Jesus took care of my particular transgressions. He paid for them with his blood as it mixed with Jerusalem topsoil at the foot of his cross. He died for my sins. He died for me.

Definite Atonement reminds you, brother or sister, that Jesus really did die for *you*. He had you, specifically, in mind. *Your* sins, from birth certificate to death certificate, were taken on and taken away by Jesus. He took your guilt. Your shame. Your death. Deliberately, specifically, consciously. You are redefined by his definite death for your specific sins. He didn't die for an undefined people whose names and identities he did not know. He died for his flock, whom he knows by name, and he hung there for each of them, knowing them, loving them. He knew all of your faults, sins, and ridiculousness, and he still let nails be hammered into his hands and feet because of his love for you. You can say, with Paul, that "Christ ... loved me and gave himself for me" (Galatians 2 v 20).

Beloved, Jesus loved you, personally, and gave himself for you, definitely.

The moment the Definite Atonement of the Lord Jesus hits our hearts, and is more than a dividing line in our doctrinal debates, is the moment we can more fully appreciate the atonement. It is unparalleled, knock-you-back love. As John Piper says:

"God does not mean for the bride of his Son [the church] to only feel loved with general, world-embracing love. He means for her to feel ravished with the specificity of his affection that he set on her before the world existed. He means for us to feel a focused: 'I chose you. And I sent my Son to die to have you.'"[31]

God's particular and pointed love humbles us in new ways. We see God's love for his people—the bride, the church, the flock—and we learn how to love one another from this love that loved us first. "Love consists in this: not that we loved God, but that he loved us and sent his Son to be the atoning sacrifice for our sins. Dear friends, if God loved us in this way, we also must love one another" (1 John 4 v 10-11). If God loved us specifically, we are to love one another not only unconditionally but specifically, practically, personally. We don't operate with a vague, positive sense that we love people, love humanity, love the world. We operate out of a specific

31 *Five Points*, page 52.

sense of loving the person in front of us. We are going to love beyond aspiration and attitude. We must love in action because Jesus did more than recognize that the cross was needed—he hung on it, bled on it, and died on it. Love involves specifics, tangibility, sacrifice.

The faces we see on Sunday—people smiling and serving— we must love beyond a foggy sense of obligated love. We must love our fellow church members with specificity. You must be committed to serving, praying for, and encouraging the people precisely placed in your life by God.

Here is one simple, meaningful thing you could do: learn the names of the people in your church. Remember them. Call them by name. No more "Hey... brother." Their name is written down in the Lamb's book of life—let it be on your mind and heart too. If you forget a name—as I often do— humble yourself and say, "I'm sorry, can you tell me your name again?" Love leads us to truly know one another. If we know the definite design of the atonement but there is no definite love among us, we have misunderstood the design of the atonement. Or, to put it another way, we have "L" in our head but not in our heart.

And don't stop there. Paul tells us how the sure sin-paying death of Christ should transform us in our day-to-day love for one another:

> "Adopt the same attitude as that of Christ Jesus, who, existing in the form of God, did not consider equality with God as something to be exploited. Instead he

emptied himself by assuming the form of a servant, taking on the likeness of humanity. And when he had come as a man, he humbled himself by becoming obedient to the point of death—even to death on a cross." (Philippians 2 v 5-8)

The humble attitude and action of Christ and his cross is now available to us. He didn't exploit his Godness. He didn't use his position and power for an ego trip. Instead, he served us till he became a cold corpse on the cross. We have a true heart-knowing of the atoning love of Christ when these attitudes take root and blossom in our lives.

How many times has a Christian leader exploited their position of power or their social-media platform for their own good? How many times has a Five-Point Calvinist exploited their knowledge for their own ego? How many times have we rattled off sound theology but refused to stop and pray for someone, or hesitated to get dirt under our nails to serve someone? How many times have aspiring pastors passed up teaching at the retirement center or the third-grade Sunday-school class because they only want the big stage? Definite Atonement, the death-blow to our sins, must also be the death-blow to our pride. We can't be the kinds of people who love the letter of the atonement but neglect the spirit of it. The definite atonement of Christ brings a definite humility to our lives, seen in acts of specific, sacrificial service.

Reflecting on this new attitude that we have in Christ, Paul says we should "Do nothing out of selfish ambition or conceit, but in humility consider others as more important than yourselves. Everyone should look out not only for his own interests, but also for the interests of others" (Philippians 2 v 3-4). A real Calvinist is a humble, servant-hearted Calvinist.

A true knowledge of the atonement leads you beyond conversations on the extent of the atonement—it leads you to ask your pastors and church leaders to what extent you can serve your church. Keep walking past debate halls and into the hall where the children of your church are taught. Clean the bathrooms, pass out bulletins, help people park, wash the coffee pots. The specificity of the atonement calls for specific humble acts of service in the body of Christ.

If you see people stacking chairs and picking up trash after a Sunday morning service and your instinct is to stay occupied with your breezy conversation, you can know that definite atonement definitely hasn't humbled you to the point of death to self, and looking to the interests and needs of others. The wires from the head to the heart aren't connected.

The effect of the atonement on daily life is practical; it is connected to the nitty-gritty of life. It helps us to not jockey for the front seat of the car, or to pout when we don't get to go to the restaurant we wanted or when our spouse would rather watch another singing competition or superhero flick. The cross teaches us—compels us—to consider the interests of others.

Let me tell you one place where definite atonement must make a difference to me. When I'm in my car with my kids, four-year-old Oliver only wants to listen to the Mickey Mouse Clubhouse soundtrack. Every time. I've curated some great jazz playlists. Nope. He wants Mickey Mouse. And I have to remind myself that definite atonement is definitely relevant for this moment. Since Jesus specifically, deliberately served me even as it led to his death, I am to put my son's interest above my own. I must. The humble attitude of Christ isn't mere wishful thinking; it's my new operating system.

Definite atonement flows into our humility, our attitudes, our actions.

A DEFINITE COMMITMENT TO UNITY

Sadly, Five-Pointers can be some of the least unifying people. But Definite Atonement teaches us to love and honor all of Christ's sheep, regardless of how "Reformed" their views are. There is "one flock, one shepherd" (John 10 v 16)—and that ranks higher than our many theological camps, tribes, and conferences. We mishandle Definite Atonement if we establish it as a line for fellowship. In fact, we misunderstand it. If I believe that Jesus deliberately died for the sins of every single person who places their trust in him—if I understand that he knew the name of every member of the flock for which he died—how can I be anything less than totally committed to the unity of that flock? Believing in the definite nature of the atonement means we should have a definite love for the unity of all of Christ's people. Christ's people are Christ's people, whether they sign off on Definite Atonement or not. Definite Atonement expands the borders of our love toward all of Christ's redeemed sheep. Jesus unites us.

The Lord, not Limited Atonement, defines our fellowship. The sureness of Christ's death should create a solid love for one another—the local church, the global church, and the persecuted church. The people you see on Sunday morning, as they hold the bread and drink the cup—they are your family because of the work of Christ. We should love gospel-stewarding churches all around the world, filled with languages we've never heard and skin colors not our own, because they are family in Christ. We love the whole church, the whole bride, all of Christ's people.

You can—and should—have meaningful fellowship and ministry with believers who don't see eye to eye on the extent of the atonement. Jesus' flock is his flock because he is their Shepherd—their Leader and their Protector and their Provider. The flock are those—five-pointers, four-pointers, no-pointers, and never-heard-of-these-pointers—who agree that Christ alone saves. The boundaries of the sheep pen are marked out by faith in the Lord Jesus, not by number-boards signifying how many points you sign up to.

I have dear friends in ministry who hold to different practices concerning baptism, frequency and availability of the Lord's Supper, women deacons, the continuation of prophecy, and the extent of the atonement—but I've never thought to break fellowship, argue till they agree with me, or make fun of them behind their backs. We love each other. So, we make wisecracks to each others' faces. We are united in Christ above all. The extent of our oneness in Christ supersedes any disagreement on the range of the atonement.

If your Christian friends, small-group members, pastor, seminary professor, spouse, boyfriend or girlfriend, or family members hold to a different understanding on the extent of atonement—don't become conceited (Philippians 2 v 3). Satan would love for us to find pride in how we understand the humble cross of Christ. Don't give in. Consider every Arminian, every Four-Pointer, every Christian as more important than yourself. Don't look down on them. Look for ways you can love them and serve them, regardless of whether they are fully "Calvinized." Christ, not Calvinism, is all.

Every sheep believes in the atonement. We are all trusting the same risen Lord. Any other source for unity is an alternative source of righteousness. There is no righteousness in being a five-pointer. Righteousness is found in Christ alone. Only. Always. Christ's people all agree that Jesus is the only Lord and Savior. God saves sinners—on that point we can humbly agree to agree.

6. DRAWN IN AND SENT OUT

Cheesecake has never done me wrong. I've had subpar brownies. Concrete-like cookies are a major bummer. But even the worst cheesecake is still pretty tasty.

When we go out to eat, if cheesecake is on the menu, Natalie knows I'm getting it. My abs would be more washboardy if I weren't so drawn to cheesecake. But I can't help it. Natalie, on the other hand, can say no to the cream-cheese delicacy without batting an eye—yet if creme brûlée is on the menu, she accepts her fate.

Maybe you approach dessert in a restaurant as an open-handed issue; you don't have a preference till you know all the options. Not us. We are what we are—Mr. Cheesecake and Mrs. Creme Brûlée. We want what we want—well, we did until something happened.

While enjoying a tower of seafood in Newport Beach, California, with the ocean in view, it was time to think about dessert. I joked about my usual order with Natalie, but then the guy at the table next to us butted in: "Hey, I heard you say you are getting cheesecake. Don't. I'm serious. This restaurant is known for its warm butter cake topped with a giant scoop of vanilla ice cream. You have to get it." I smiled, said OK, and thanked him for the tip. When the server came by to take our dessert order, Mr. Interrupter was still at the table next to us. I had to order the warm butter cake. I caved under the pressure… and I wish I could find the man who leaned on my table that day so I could wash his feet. The first bite of that butter cake was the single best bite of my life. Cheesecake schmeesechake. Crème bru-nevermind. Our dessert desires have been flipped by the butter cake gospel. Natalie and I have tasted and seen.

Now if total depravity is true, *and* unconditional election is true, then what takes a person, spiritually speaking, from cheesecake to warm butter cake—from wills bent on our own empire-building to wills on fire for God's glory? How did we move from unbelief to belief, from death to life? We taste and see that the Lord is good (Psalm 34 v 8). He illumines our tastebuds. Which is also known as: Irresistible Grace.

The reason you believed the gospel isn't because you figured it all out one night. Your faith didn't bloom because your mind worked out that belief in Jesus was a no-brainer.

Irresistible Grace means that God took our deaf, blind, and stubborn hearts and made them hear, see, and respond to the gospel call. We didn't become Christians on our own. Christians are Christians because of God.

The apostle John reminds us how people believe in Jesus. It's because Jesus "gave ... the right to be children of God, to those who believe in his name, who were born, not of natural descent, or of the will of the flesh, or of the will of man, but of God" (John 1 v 12-13). God is the cause; he makes us his children. And every Christian instinctively knows this is true. Have you ever heard anyone thank themselves for their conversion, their new life, or the forgiveness of sins? Never. We always thank God. Instinctively, we know God is the cause of our new life, our faith, our born again-ness. It wasn't our will, our work, our anything. *Soli* Deo gloria, as the Reformers put it—it's all to the glory of God *alone*.

GOD CALLS

The labor and delivery room is a memorable room. The memories of my children entering the world, Natalie's unmatched smile as she held them, and even their shrieks and screams as they flexed their vocal chords all remind me of the gospel of the kingdom of God. Like a newborn baby whose first act on leaving the womb is to cry out, a sign of life, so the newborn Christian lets out their first cry from the new heart of their new life: "Jesus, you saved me! Thank you, Lord!" As Peter tells us, "Because of his great mercy he has given us new birth" (1 Peter 1 v 3). God gives it. You cannot give birth to yourself. And without it, you cannot see the kingdom of God (John 3 v 3). The sovereign Lord rewires our hearts, calls us, and brings us out from the tomb. It's the work of the triune God. The Father elects, the Son atones, and the Spirit calls.

Jesus gives us a meteorological lesson to teach us a theological and doxological lesson: "The wind blows where it pleases, and you hear its sound, but you don't know where it comes from or where it is going. So it is with everyone born of the Spirit" (John 3 v 8). The reason you believe the crucifixion of a man from Nazareth back in AD 33 prepaid the penalty for your sins is because the Holy Spirit put his wind in the sails of your soul. He moved you from death to life, from darkness to light. The Spirit took what the Father did for you in eternity past, and what the Son did for you that glorious weekend in Jerusalem, and he applied it to you here and now. The Spirit will keep calling sinners to new life, and there is no rejecting this call.

There are two kinds of calls that ring out in the gospel message. The general call, or external call, goes out to everyone who is listening to the sermon, reading the Bible, or hearing someone share the gospel in an Uber. *Come and believe in Jesus.* And then there is an undetectable effectual call, or internal call, which is a work of the Holy Spirit causing people to respond with faith in Christ. The general call can be resisted and rejected. The effectual call is irresistible. God doesn't fail. His RSVPs on this invitation are always 100% yes. "The external call alone would be insufficient," says John Calvin, "did not God effectually draw to himself those whom he has called."[32]

The Spirit shows you the glories of the gospel and you agree. Glorious. When the Spirit goes to work, he brings you to the moment when you believe. You are convinced. You have faith. The grace is irresistible. When, back in the beginning, God said, "Let there be light," there was light. And when he said it was time for the gospel light to flood your heart, there was light. "For God who said, 'Let light shine out of darkness,' has shone in our hearts to give the light of the knowledge of God's glory in the face of Jesus Christ" (2 Corinthians 4 v 6). When Jesus told Lazarus to come out of his tomb, Lazarus walked out (John 11 v 44)—musty graveclothes and all. And when you were dead in your sins, he called you with the gospel, and he made you alive in Christ.

THE SPIRIT DRAWS

Why do two unbelieving people who come from the same background, even the same family, hear the same sermon and respond differently? It's not because one is smarter, or savvier, or more spiritual. It's because one is experiencing the work of God, drawing them in.

The gravitational pull of God's grace is how and why people respond to the gospel. "No one can come to me

---

32 John Calvin and James Anderson, *Commentary on the Book of Psalms*, Vol. 3, page 322.

unless the Father who sent me draws him, and I will raise him up on the last day" (John 6 v 44). You walked an aisle, prayed with your parents or your pastor, or believed while hearing a sermon because the Father pulled you toward Christ. He caused you to be born again. God is the reason we believe. His kindness to us leaves us singing his praises.

Do you feel the compounding and humbling effect of Calvinism here? The Father elected you in spite of you, the Son died for you when you didn't ask him to, and then it's not like you connected the dots on your own, placed your faith in Jesus, and found a seat on the train to glory. No, the Spirit drew you. Faith is a gift (Ephesians 2 v 8-9). We often think of salvation as a train waiting at the station. Prepaid tickets are offered, seats are available, and the people with enough sense—people like us—get on board before the last call. Wrong. God lifted us from our deadness, like a mama lion picking up her cubs by their scruff, and he took us to the station and buckled us in our seats. He did it all.

KEEP SPEAKING—I HAVE PEOPLE IN THIS CITY

Hyper-Calvinism isn't a compliment. It sounds like one, but it is an erroneous teaching that downplays evangelism, church-planting, and going to the nations, on the basis that God is sovereign. God is in control, and God has elected his people; so he's going to save his people whether we speak the truth or not, whether we give our money to foreign missions or not, right? It seems logical. The only problem with Hyper-Calvinism is the Bible.

When Jesus told his followers to "go, therefore, and make disciples of all nations" (Matthew 28 v 19), there weren't any asterisks or wink-winks. There are no opt-outs available in the verses telling us to make disciples, share the gospel, and go to the nations. How will they hear if we don't speak, go, proclaim (Romans 10 v 14-15)? We have a mission. And we have a supreme reason to go forward in confidence.

Knowing that God will draw his people to himself does not keep us at a safe distance to watch the show—it equips us with a bold obedience to witness to unbelievers. The apostle Paul is the proof. He met fierce resistance in many of the cities where he sought to plant the gospel. Acts 18 tells us about Paul's difficult ministry and hints at the discouragement he must have felt in the midst of it.

"When Silas and Timothy arrived from Macedonia, Paul devoted himself to preaching the word and testified to the Jews that Jesus is the Messiah. When they resisted and blasphemed, he shook out his clothes and told them, 'Your blood is on your own heads! I am innocent. From now on I will go to the Gentiles.' So he left there and went to the house of a man named Titius Justus, a worshiper of God, whose house was next door to the synagogue. Crispus, the leader of the synagogue, believed in the Lord, along with his whole household. Many of the Corinthians, when they heard, believed and were baptized."

(Acts 18 v 5-8)

Amid all the resistance and blasphemy among his own Jewish people, God was drawing people to Christ through Paul's ministry. But what happens next to Paul makes me think Paul was discouraged by what was going on. It seems that fear, or worry, or maybe frustration began to fill Paul's heart. Why do I think that? The next two verses in Acts 18 show why:

> "The Lord said to Paul in a night vision, 'Don't be afraid, but keep on speaking and don't be silent. For I am with you, and no one will lay a hand on you to hurt you, because I have many people in this city.'"
>
> (Acts 18 v 9-10)

Jesus speaks to Paul in this vision to give him two reasons to keep going, to not quiet down, and to not give in to fear. One, God is with him. *I got you.* Two, there are people in this city who God is going to save. *I got them.* The Lord is in control of Paul's life and Paul's ministry—and that's true of yours too. He is with you always (Matthew 28 v 20). He is your confidence. He is calling each Christian off the sidelines and into the heart of the mission. And the Spirit will perform his ministry through you because the wind will wisp and whisper new life where he wishes.

IRRESISTIBLE GRACE GIVES YOU COURAGE

Theologically-driven Christians are concerned with stewarding and safeguarding the message of the gospel. This is 100% right. But we can't under-prioritize the call to *spread* the gospel. In fact, we are only rightly stewarding the gospel message if we are spreading it as "far as the curse is found," as the hymn-writer Isaac Watts put it. Theologian J.I. Packer reminds us:

"Christ's command means that we all should be devoting all our resources of ingenuity and enterprise to the task of making the gospel known in every possible way to every possible person. Unconcern and inaction with regard to evangelism are always, therefore, inexcusable. And the doctrine of divine sovereignty would be grossly misapplied if we should invoke it in such a way as to lessen the urgency, and immediacy, and priority, and binding constraint, of the evangelistic imperative. No revealed truth may be invoked to extenuate sin. God did not teach us the reality of his rule in order to give us an excuse for neglecting his orders."[33]

Humble Calvinism hungers to see people meet Jesus. Irresistible Grace doesn't stifle church-planting, or hiking up a mountain to evangelize an unreached tribe, or going across the factory floor to invite a co-worker to a Bible study. It gives us a God-dependent courage and boldness to do those very things—and more!—for the cause of Christ.

Knowing the power of God's irresistible call of grace releases us from fear. Conversions to Christ don't rely on us. God is the one who draws, who awakens, who calls from the crypt. The burden isn't on our back to get the results.

---

33 J.I. Packer, *Evangelism and the Sovereignty of God*, page 38.

Christians don't close the deal. The Spirit of Christ does. Share freely. Boldly.

Often we are stunted in spreading the gospel because we are worried we don't know enough, we are unsure how to answer objections, and, sadly, we doubt there is any possibility the person in question will believe. But when we know, in our hearts, that God is the one who calls and we are his messengers, we can cut out all the objections we come up with and go forward knowing that God will accomplish his purpose. Of course we should learn how to helpfully and faithfully present the gospel—but we should never pretend that our powers of persuasion are the reason people are born again into the kingdom of God. The Spirit moves where he wishes. The power of regeneration rests with God. Here's J.I. Packer again:

> "While we must always remember that it is our responsibility to proclaim salvation, we must never forget that it is God who saves. It is God who brings men and women under the sound of the gospel, and it is God who brings them to faith in Christ. Our evangelistic work is the instrument that he uses for this purpose, but the power that saves is not in the instrument: it is in the hand of the One who uses the instrument."[34]

Hyper-Calvinism is a delusional, though comfortable, doctrine. And if you're reading this book, you're likely

---

34 *Evangelism and the Sovereignty of God,* page 32.

not a Hyper-Calvinist. But beware—Hoax-Calvinism is even worse.

Can you remember the last time you shared the gospel with someone in a place that wasn't a church building? What is their name? Would you panic if your child wanted to evangelize an unreached people group in a dangerous part of the Middle East? Hoax-Calvinism condemns Hyper-Calvinism as unbiblical, which it is, but then mimics Hyper-Calvinism by never putting boots on the ground, never befriending unbelievers, and only begrudgingly, at best, telling people about Jesus. Who have you asked the Lord to save? Is there a detectable passion for the spread of the gospel—not just good gospel doctrine—in your life? Avoid Hoax-Calvinism at all costs. It snarls at Hyper-Calvinism in public but then sympathizes with it in private. Any version of Calvinism that lacks zeal for the lost is a counterfeit. It's hypocritical. Real Calvinism runs on a Great Commission passion for the glory of God and the joy of all peoples in Christ the Lord.

COME WATCH GOD AT WORK

Knowing Irresistible Grace makes living on mission irresistible. God will do his work through our work. We plant. Another waters. God gives the growth (1 Corinthians 3 v 6-7). We can trust God to grow his vineyard, and we can thank God that we get to work in it. So we sow seeds. We water everywhere we can, whenever we can, because there is no conservation effort in the conversion effort. And as we witness to the lost, we witness God do his work.

I've seen this firsthand. I worked at Starbucks for a few years while working at a church part-time, and I hated it. I wrongly thought Starbucks was just a stepping stone for ministry. I was ready for "real ministry" at a church. Puttering around making coffee and spending time with unbelievers seemed like a waste of my time and talents. I'm so glad God changed my thinking. One way or another, I came to realize I had a ministry and a mission right there behind the counter. While making frappuccinos and other overpriced coffee-related items, I began to talk to my co-workers about Jesus with questions like "Who do you think Jesus is?" and "What do you think Christianity is all about?" and, my favorite, "What do you think Jesus is doing right now?" Gospel conversations and friendships were brewing.

While talking about Jesus with one of my Buddhist co-workers, she happily told me, "I forgot to tell you! I'm becoming a Christian in two days."

My head snapped back as I said, "What? You are? How are you doing that in two days?"

"I'm going to a Catholic church and taking a class."

I smiled and said, "Can I tell you something? You don't have to do that to become a Christian."

She was surprised and asked, "Really? Well, what should I do to get saved?"—I'm not kidding; this actually happened.

Instead of rushing her to "make a decision" as we were

shuffling drinks out the drive-thru window, I said, "Why don't you come over for dinner tonight, and my wife and I will tell you how we became Christians, and how you can become one too?" She agreed and couldn't wait to have spaghetti with us.

After dinner, we sat around the table and talked about faith in Jesus, his cross, his empty tomb, forgiveness of sins, and more. But we weren't getting the traction I was hoping for—until an idea hit me. I grabbed three Bibles, opened them all up to Ephesians 2, explained a little bit about the letter, and told her to ask anything she wanted as we read. We read about being dead in our sins, God's mercy, and being saved by grace through faith—and then she started laughing. Giggling.

Hesitantly, I asked her, "Why are you laughing?"

She looked up from the Bible with a giant smile: "I'm so happy because I just became a Christian. If Jesus did all of this for me, I believe. Buddha didn't do anything for me. I want Jesus."

Amen, sister. Amen.

When I think about her conversion to Christ, it always reminds me of two things: God's calling is irresistible, and he chooses to work through instruments. My wife and I did very little—other times with other friends, we did more and saw nothing but confusion or rejection. All we did on this occasion was to ask our friend a question, tell her a truth, invite her over for dinner, and read Ephesians 2.

And the Lord called her through it. Not because we were great, but because he is.

Paul saw this as he evangelized a group of women in Philippi. One of them was called Lydia, and "the Lord opened her heart to respond to what Paul was saying" (Acts 16 v 14). Paul spoke. The Spirit worked. Unless the Lord opens the heart, the gospel message will ricochet off its wrought-iron gates. But when he does open the heart, the gospel becomes irresistible. Always. As Calvin describes it, "He must therefore call us to him before we call upon him; we can have no access till he first invite us."[35]

God's sovereign call doesn't mean we have to limit how broad or sincerely we proclaim the promise of the gospel. While preaching in Matthew 11, Jesus puts irresistible grace and the free proclamation of the gospel side by side. "No one knows the Son except the Father, and no one knows the Father except the Son and anyone to whom the Son desires to reveal him" (Matthew 11 v 27). God's sovereign call is the reason why anyone believes, so, "Come to me, all of you who are weary and burdened, and I will give you rest" (Matthew 11 v 28). The gospel is offered to everyone because God can draw anyone. Our mission, empowered by the Spirit, is to tell people, "If you are weary, burned out from life, exhausted— go to Jesus. Look to him. See the cross and a stack of folded-up graveclothes. Come to him. He welcomes you."

---

35 John Calvin and William Pringle, *Commentary on the Book of the Prophet Isaiah,* Vol. 2, page 74.

Whoever comes, God brought them in. He woos our wills according to his will—and God's invited you to work alongside him.

COME JOIN WITH GOD'S WORK

My son loves to help me. If I'm taking out the recycling, he'll run outside: "I wanna help. Let me help." When Natalie comes back from the grocery store, he loves to help unload what he can with those four-year-old biceps. Oliver will help feed the dogs, throw away trash, or put dishes in the sink. I asked him why he insists on helping so much, and he responded in his adorable quasi-lisp, "You're my Papa. So I help you. That's what I do." That's what he does. He knows his identity comes with an activity. *I'm your son, so I serve.* He's got a mission—to be my co-worker. And he loves it.

In 1 Corinthians 3, Paul gives us what is one of the most stop-you-in-your-tracks verses. He gives himself, Peter, and Apollos a title that rattles my theological neurons: "We are God's coworkers" (1 Corinthians 3 v 9). He says the same of his younger protégé, Timothy, whom he describes as "our brother and God's coworker in the gospel of Christ" (1 Thessalonians 3 v 2). Wait—God has coworkers?! Why? He's all-powerful, never-tiring, and omnicompetent. We sleep for a third of our lives, suffer from seasonal allergies, and forget where we put our car keys. And yet, like those early Christians, we are God's coworkers in proclaiming the gospel of Christ.

God doesn't need us as his coworkers—he isn't lacking the strength or ability to spread the fame of his name or to call his people to faith in him. Just like when I'm unloading the groceries, Oliver and I will each take a side of the crate-sized package of paper towels; he strains with all he's got while I smile and thank him for helping me out. I could do it by myself. Honestly, he's not bearing much of the load. But I love it when he helps because I love him. I want him to help. He's a part of the family.

Well, God's invited his children to work in the family business. He's given us an activity from the identity we have in Christ—coworkers for the fame of Christ. He's empowered us with the Spirit to do just that (Acts 1 v 8). When we live on mission, spread the gospel, and strike up conversations about the crucified and risen Christ, God is working in us and with us and through us. The Lord is with you. And you cannot fail to do the good works he's prepared for you (Ephesians 2 v 10). Sure, he could do it all himself. Sure, he'll call his people. But he chooses to let you participate in the greatest business on earth—bringing people from darkness to light, from hell to heaven.

Who is Jesus directing you to evangelize? Is the Lord calling you to the nations? Is church-planting where the compass keeps pointing? What keeps you from taking the next steps? For the love of God and your neighbor, don't let Calvinism be the caution tape. Go forward with a courageous Christ-proclaiming and Spirit-dependent Calvinism as the supporting steel beams of your mission.

Maybe you've heard the phrase "Work like an Arminian and sleep like a Calvinist." In other words, "Work as though it depends on you, and sleep as though it depends on God." Well, I want to say, don't do that. Don't do ministry and missions as if it rests on you. Work *and* sleep like a Calvinist. Work like it is all up to the most powerful person in the universe. Work like you are God's humble coworker, pointing people to the person and work of Jesus Christ. Go to the nations, evangelize your friends, and plant churches because you know God is sovereign. Be a hard-working, expectantly-evangelizing Calvinist who trusts God's sovereignty. Work hard for the glory of God. And enjoy watching what he lets you be a part of.

CALVINISTS ON MISSION

Real Calvinism is humble Calvinism, and humble Calvinism is missional Calvinism. It was like this right from the start.

John Calvin was a titan of theology and missions. He wasn't a theologian who double-bolted himself in his study. Calvin was a pastor, a theologian, and a church-planting strategist. While Calvin pastored in Geneva, he also aggressively helped plant churches throughout France:

"By 1555, Calvin and his Geneva supporters had planted five churches in France. Four years later, they had planted 100 churches in France. By 1562, Calvin's Geneva, with the help of some of their sister cities, had planted more than 2,000 churches in France. Calvin was the leading church planter in Europe. He led the way in every part of the process: he trained, assessed, sent, counseled, corresponded with, and prayed for the missionaries and church planters he sent."[36]

Old-school Calvinism was a missional Calvinism—and the best of the "New Calvinism" is too. Or, it should be. I pray that John Piper will be proved right when he says, "The New Calvinism is aggressively mission-driven, including missional impact on social evils, evangelistic impact in personal networks, and missionary impact on the unreached peoples of the world."[37]

I see this holy ambition at work in the Acts 29 church-planting network. Acts 29 is a diverse, global family of church-planting churches that believes God is sovereign in saving sinners—and believes we should engage the culture, live on mission, and plant churches in hard places like the Middle East or the slums of global cities. In their 2018 Annual Report, there were 674 churches in Acts 29 with $23 million pledged by these churches to go toward church-planting. Over forty countries are represented in these churches—Australia, Burkina-Faso, Chile, Democratic Republic of Congo, India, Japan, Kenya, Lebanon, Malawi, Mozambique, Pakistan,

36 John Starke, "John Calvin, Missionary and Church Planter" on The Gospel Coalition blog, https://www.thegospelcoalition.org/article/john-calvin-missionary-and-church-planter/

37 John Piper, "The New Calvinism and the New Community" on Desiring God blog, https://www.desiringgod.org/messages/the-new-calvinism-and-the-new-community

Romania, Slovakia, Turkey, United Arab Emirates, Uganda, and more—and you'll hear gospel-centered sermons delivered in 23 different languages across the network of churches.[38] These are amazing works of God done in the confidence of God's grace to call sinners to himself. And that's just one example, one network.

Calvinism doesn't inhibit mission. It ignites it. Real Calvinism has always been a catalyst for church-planting. Jesus will build his church. And he will call his people through his people. He did in Corinth 2,000 years ago. And he will on your street today.

Old Calvinism and New Calvinism both know this: God's grace is irresistible. A high view of God's call in saving sinners should lead to a high view of God's call in sending us out with the message of salvation. He called you to believe and he called you to make disciples. The Spirit caused you to be born again. He caused you to be his humble coworker in the spread of his name. You don't need to join the mission—you are already in it. Calvinists are to be humble and hungry evangelists—not despite the doctrine but because of it. God's calling is irresistible. We are his instruments. And that calling is irrevocable—which is where we turn in the next chapter.

---

38 Acts 29 2018 Annual Report, http://publications.acts29.com/annual-report-2018#!/stats

7. HE HOLDS
OUR HANDS

As a baby, my daughter was an all-time awful sleeper. For months, Natalie and I were zombies. And then, when Ivy finally got the hang of sleeping, another enemy to peaceful sleep invaded our house. Nightmares. When we'd hear Ivy crying in fear and dread in her sleep I'd rush in, swoop her up and say, "I got you. It's okay. I got you." She would hold my thumb as I held onto her.

We've been out of the nightmare stage with Ivy for a while, but my son is now in the don't-run-off-because-there-are-cars-around phase. So when I go to the grocery store and I get Oliver out of the truck, I tell him, "Hold my hand, bud. You can't run off. There are cars driving all around here, and they could run you over and hurt you. Stay with me." I tell him the truth about parking lots and cars because I love him—and he must trust and obey me. But of course, though I tell Oliver to hold my hand, it's more significant that I'm holding on to him than that he is holding on to me. While we are holding each other's hands, my hand-hold on his left hand keeps him far safer than his toy Mickey Mouse's in his right hand. His tiny hand could lose its grip on me. But I won't lose my grip on him. I'm not letting him go. As we walk past every car, wait for cars backing up, and patiently wait on the crosswalk, he's safe in his father's hand.

Like my baby girl holding onto my thumb, and my son holding my hand in the parking lot, we are holding hands with our heavenly Father as we walk through life. But what matters far more is that our Father is holding onto ours. We are eternally secure. "No one will snatch them out of my hand," Jesus said. "My Father, who has given them to me, is greater than all. No one is able to snatch them out of the Father's hand. I and the Father are one" (John 10 v 28-30). Satan can't rip you out of the hands of God, and you can't slip out of his grip. No one and nothing can separate you from the love of God. "For I am persuaded that neither death nor life, nor angels nor rulers, nor things present nor things to come, nor powers, nor height nor depth, nor any other created thing will be able to separate us from the love of God that is in Christ Jesus our Lord" (Romans 8 v 38-39).

YOU CAN'T BE UNBORN

The last petal of TULIP teaches us one of the most comforting and assuring truths in the world: you cannot lose your salvation. As Paul put it, "I am sure of this, that he who started a good work in you will carry it on to completion until the day of Christ Jesus" (Philippians 1 v 6). The Puritan writer John Flavel wrote of that verse in 1691, "Did Christ finish his work for us? Then there can be no doubt, but he will also finish his work in us."[39] Perseverance of the Saints means that believers in Christ will make it home to the new heavens and the new earth, and will reign forever with Christ, because of Christ.

Believers will not—cannot!—"un-believe." Will there be doubts? Certainly. Will we sin? Yes. Will there be periods of backsliding into sin and a belittling of God's grace? Probably. But prodigals eventually come home. Sins that have already been covered by the blood of Jesus cannot be uncovered. And this verse is always true: "There is now no condemnation for those in Christ Jesus" (Romans 8 v 1). The timestamp on this verse speaks volumes. *Now*. There is an ever-present "nowness" to our status in Christ. Right now, in Christ, you are un-condemnable. From when you first believed, to this moment, and months from now when you are struggling with assurance—in all of those nows, there is no condemnation. Forgiveness of sins will never be taken back. If you've been born again, you can't be unborn. If you've been raised to new life with Christ, he won't wave you off like a mosquito and throw you back in the tomb. The promise of eternal life won't be renegotiated.

---

39 John Flavel, *The Complete Works of John Flavel*, Vol. 1, page 437.

LOSING MY CHILD (AND HOW GOD IS NOT LIKE ME)

If I could tally how many sunglasses, debit cards, and credit cards Natalie has lost, this book would double in size. While writing this section, I kid you not, my dear wife texted and asked if I would order her another card because she lost it. But her ability to lose things is nothing compared to mine.

I lost one of our kids.

A few years ago, I took Ivy and Oliver to the movie theater to see *Finding Dory*, but it turned into *Finding Ivy*. Oliver was potty-training at the time and at the end of the movie he had a minor accident. I leaned over to Ivy and said, "As soon as the movie is done, let's run down the stairs, and get home. Oliver had an accident." The credits roll, I pick up Oliver, run down the chunky theater stairs, and I wait at the bottom for Ivy.

I don't see her.

I'm bobbing my head between the shoulders of adults, and I still don't see her. I change strategies and look at people's feet, hoping I can spot her pink Toms. Nothing.

I panic. *Maybe I missed her. Maybe she's outside already. I should have held her hand.* I run as fast as I can while jostling a slightly damp two-year-old. I scan the hallway for my little girl and her pink shoes.

I hear crying.

I can't find my dad. I'm lost.

I whip around and see my girl, talking through tears to an employee. My anxiety and fear give way to relief and shame. *There's the guy who lost his own daughter. Yup. That's me.*

Most of us are apt to misplace, lose, or forget important things (though maybe not your kids)—and so without a heart-grasp of the Perseverance of the Saints, this is how we will view our salvation. What if we lose it? What if we stop holding onto it? What if we don't make it? But we need to lose the view of salvation that sees our faith like Ivy at the movies—like it's all up to us to keep hold of our salvation and not lose it. In reality, *we* are Ivy. And our heavenly Father is a much better dad than me. I lost Ivy for a minute, but God never loses his kids. Ever. He's got hold of his children, and he does not lose his grip.

You will live in a constant state of fear if you think salvation can be lost. You will worry whether you are reading your Bible enough, whether you are praying enough, or whether you might just sin too many times and salvation is going to slip through your fingers. God wants to lift that burden off of you. It's not yours to carry.

You can't have confidence in your ability to keep your faith and secure your salvation. And you don't need to. There is no room for pride in preserving grace. Confident assurance is found in Christ. The reason we stay Christians is not that we are great at being Christians. You know who's great at living like Christ? Christ. He is our assurance. If you could lose your salvation, it'd already be missing. You wouldn't have made it through a single day. You wouldn't have made it to the next meal. If the security of our salvation depends on our performance and our efforts alone, we are doomed. But it depends on Jesus, and so we have hope, assurance, and a reason to rejoice. He cannot fail.

Don't link assurance to being a lover of theology, being a good Christian parent, or being a pastor. If you do, what will happen when you aren't able to hang with the latest theological argument circling on the internet? When you aren't being a rockstar parent? When your season of pastoral ministry ends? Don't look for assurance of salvation in your Bible-reading plan, the behavior of your kids, or the signature on your email—that's works-security. Don't try to sneak in your works to stabilize your heart before God. Christ alone is your final assurance. You may lose the ability to hang in certain circles, you may lose your temper in the grocery store, and you may lose your ministry—but you cannot lose Christ, because he will not lose you. Live with a humble confidence that you will make it to the end, not because you'll earn it but because God will keep you from stumbling because you are connected to Christ (Jude v 24).

BEYOND PANIC AND PRIDE

What are the alternatives to a Christ-gazing humble confidence? Panic or pride. Panic wells up when we are struggling in our walk and forget that it depends on

Christ. *I won't make it. I'm a failure. I've messed up one too many times. I should have worked this out by now.* Pride rises up when we are doing well and forget that it depends on Christ. *I'm good at being a Christian. Why does everyone else struggle so much? I don't understand why people can't— well—be a bit more like me. It's not that hard!* But a true understanding of the Perseverance of the Saints points us to Christ as our confidence—as the vine from whom we bear any and all spiritual fruit, including our faith. No pride. No panic. Perseverance is found in the person of Christ.

One of the reasons we lack assurance in the Christian life is because we often view salvation as a certificate of acceptance with God. We have the papers, they are authentic, and we move on. All we have to do is not lose that certificate so that we can present it on the last day. But salvation isn't a certificate of acceptance—salvation is connection to Christ. It's baptism into Christ. It's an ongoing gift of faith that abides in, endures because of, and enjoys knowing Christ. To be in Christ is what it means to be saved. "This is why I endure all things for the elect: so that they also may obtain salvation, which is in Christ Jesus, with eternal glory" (2 Timothy 2 v 10).

Salvation = being in Christ. "For the wages of sin is death, but the gift of God is eternal life in Christ Jesus our Lord" (Romans 6 v 23).

Eternal life = being in Christ. Union with Christ is the underwriting of your eternity.

Rehearse the glories of the gospel, and there you find why you will persevere till the end. You are forever accepted by God because Christ is accepted. You are declared righteous because Christ is righteous. You are made a coheir with Christ because you are forever connected to him. Your "in-Christness" is your eternal security. He will never lose his spot at the Father's right hand, and he will never lose any of his sheep. "This is the will of him who sent me: that I should lose none of those he has given me but should raise them up on the last day" (John 6 v 39). The Father's will for the Son is for him to carry you all the way to resurrection day. Lock it in. Marcus Peter Johnson captures this reality: "To say that we are preserved in Christ means that once we have been joined to him, he continues to hold us close to him and promises to never let us go."[40] Christ himself is why we are saved and stay saved. While the phrase "once saved, always saved" is easy to remember, we can do better: *once in Christ, always in Christ.*

We persevere because God preserves. Paul tells us, as J.B. Phillips translates:

"He will keep you steadfast in the faith to the end, so that when his day comes you need fear no condemnation. God is utterly dependable, and it is he who has called you into fellowship with his Son Jesus Christ, our Lord." (1 Corinthians 1 v 8-9, Phillips)

40 Marcus Peter Johnson, *One with Christ: An Evangelical Theology of Salvation*, pages 170-171.

Do you know why you didn't reject Christ yesterday? God kept you. Do you know why you won't reject Christ tomorrow? God will be keeping you. You can work out your salvation with fruitfulness and endurance and long-term faithfulness—with humble confidence—because God is at work in you.

"We persevere in grace," says R.C. Sproul, "because God perseveres in his love toward us."[41] The Father who chose you before the foundation of the world, the Son who paid for your sins on the cross, and the Spirit who caused you to be born again are all unified in securing your whole salvation. God has not only secured the verdict of justification, but also your sanctification, resurrection, glorification, and your inheritance to come (Romans 8 v 30). God has ordained the end and the means to the end. He will conform you into the image of his Son.

CONFIDENCE, BUT NOT COMPLACENCY

Perseverance of the Saints can prevent both panic and pride, but it won't lead to humble confidence until it hits our hearts. If perseverance of the saints remains head-knowledge alone, it will provoke complacency instead of confidence.

Here's how that plays out in your head as you view your own life: *Well, God will keep me. I know he's got me, and it's all about him. I'm humble enough to understand it's not up to*

---

41 R.C. Sproul, *What is Reformed Theology? Understanding the Basics*, page 211.

me. So OK, this repeated sin, it's wrong, I know that—but it doesn't threaten my salvation. God's got me. So OK, I haven't read God's word for, well, weeks, but it's not about Bible-reading. I know that. God will keep me persevering!

And here's how complacency sounds as you view other Christians around you: *Gary's not been in church for a while now. His wife says he's turned his back on the faith. Clearly he was never saved anyway.*

Kate seems to be really struggling to put Christ first. I guess it must be hard for her, what with the young kids and the unbelieving husband and the part-time job and her health issues. So good to know God's got her. She'll be fine.

No, no. Persevering in Christ isn't a free pass to lukewarmness toward the Lord and passivity when it comes to our sin and others' struggles. This doctrine is not meant to merely be an explanation of what is happening when someone falls away or finds following Christ very hard. It is certainly not intended to be an excuse for not doing anything. Even the very phrase "Perseverance of the Saints" tells you there's no room for complacency. Here's why.

PERSEVERANCE AS A *SAINT*

First, we're talking about Perseverance of the *Saints*. Saints aren't restricted to people depicted in stained glass or religious icons throughout European basilicas, or to those declared a saint by the Pope. Saints greet you on Sunday mornings. You'll find saints selling insurance, working an office job, at home raising their kids, or driving a delivery truck. Every Christian is a saint.

"Saints" is one of Paul's favorite descriptions of Christians. You'll often see this word at the beginning of his letters to the churches. It means "holy ones" or "set-apart ones." You don't become a saint through a church-ordered sainthoodery. You became a saint, a holy one, when you were united by faith to the Lord Jesus, the Holy One of Israel. "Saints" is who we are and it is how we are to live. We persevere as holy ones, and we pursue holiness as holy ones.

The truth of eternal security doesn't mean we take our foot off of the pedal of pursuing holiness. Turning from sin, loving our church family, and obeying the word of God matter. They're the work of the Spirit in our lives—the fruit of faith. They're vital signs of those who will see the Lord: "Pursue peace with everyone, and holiness—without it no one will see the Lord" (Hebrews 12 v 14). Perseverance doesn't minimize the realities of discipleship with the risen Christ—it encourages discipleship. *Keep going. You will make it. Christ is alive in you. Behave as the person you are, in Christ.* You can affirm Perseverance of the Saints in your mind, but you know it's in your heart when you pursue holiness not because you think your faith is all up to you but because you know God will keep you going in faith. You know it's in your heart when you pursue perseverance in the preserving power of God. It's the consistent logic of the New Testament:

"Dear friends, we are God's children now, and what we will be has not yet been revealed. *We know that when he appears, we will be like him* because we will see him as he is. And *everyone who has this hope in him purifies himself* just as he is pure."

(1 John 3 v 2-3, my italics)

Saints aren't sinless. We will battle with sin till our hearts stop or the trumpet blares. But the key word is *battle*. Believers fight their sin. We may suffer a defeat, but we won't become deserters. Saints persevere in sanctification and everything that comes with it—rebuke, correction, confession, repentance, and restoration. "Work out your own salvation with fear and trembling. For it is God who is working in you both to will and to work according to his good purpose" (Philippians 2 v 12-13). Perseverance of the Saints does not give any grounds for a complacent, careless, smugly secure walk with Christ. We are called to be disciples—followers, walking forward—not people who made a decision way back when, and whose lives haven't changed since.

SPOTTING THE MARATHON RUNNER

This prompts the obvious question around perseverance: what about those who made a profession of faith, and sat in church services, but then don't endure till the end? Well, the Bible is clear: "The one who endures to the end will be saved" (Matthew 24 v 13). Imagine a marathon race. In one sense, everyone running is a marathon runner. But in another, only those who endure to the finish are marathoners—and anyone who drops out was never a marathon runner at all.

Our difficulty with processing the non-endurers in the Christian race is often because we tend to confuse "making a decision for Christ" with being a disciple of Christ. Being a disciple of Christ is more than admitting who Jesus is— demons do that all the time in the Gospels. Churches are often filled with those who have demon-like "faith." People will say Jesus is the Son of God but then never love God or others, and they slither in and out of church week after week but never hear the clomp of a cross being dragged behind them as they put their sins to death. Discipleship is more than a decision. Saying a prayer doesn't protect you from hell. Neither will a profession of faith. "Once saved, always saved?" Sure, but the Bible doesn't teach "Once professed, always protected." Jesus was very clear that "not everyone who says to me, 'Lord, Lord,' will enter the kingdom of heaven, but only the one who does the will of my Father in heaven" (Matthew 7 v 21). Discipleship is about denying ourselves as our own Lord and Savior, picking up our cross of death to self, and following Jesus as Master. And the proof is in perseverance; a continued discipleship with Christ, as new creations in Christ, is God's will for his saints.

The writer of Hebrews launches an "if" bomb when he says, "For we have become participants in Christ *if* we hold firmly until the end the reality that we had at the start" (Hebrews 3 v 14, my italics). This is a discombobulating verse. We have, already, become participants in Christ, and at the same time, we are saved *if* we persevere till the end. A complacent Christian is a contradiction. Perseverance of the Saints gives believers confidence that we will make it to the end—but it doesn't mean we have our feet propped up while we sip a cold drink. We are in the well-trodden trenches of spiritual warfare. We are running toward the finish line. Participants in Christ will persevere till the end, pursue holiness, and show what they believe by how they live because God preserves his saints. Shipwrecks of faith are moments that should bring fear and trembling to our hearts—not "I-knew-its," annoyed sighs, and tidy, theologically correct explanations. When you see the wreckage, think, as the English Reformer John Bradford said, "There, but for the grace of God, go I."

So there cannot be room for complacency, because complacency is the doorway back to pride—and God opposes the proud. He gives grace to the humbly confident (James 4 v 6-7). The humbly confident prayer of the Christian is, "God, keep me from stumbling today! Give me faith today, God! You are my hope!" Are you trusting, loving, and desiring to obey Jesus today? Then you can be humbly confident that you will persevere until the day you see him face to face.

PERSEVERANCE WITH THE SAINTS (PLURAL)

There is no room for complacency because we are *saints*, called to live holy lives and called to keep walking in faith. And second, there is no room for complacency because this doctrine is the Perseverance of the SaintS. Plural. Not singular. God's given an ecosystem for the saints to persevere in—one another.

I'm no fitness buff, but there is something encouraging about exercising with a friend. I can run longer. I'm more determined to keep going. By myself, I'll give up without any internal debate. As soon as the thought "Stop" pops up, I think, "Finally, a good idea." And I'm done. But the presence of a friend pushes me. *One more lap. One more set. Faster. Let's go.* The presence of others encourages perseverance. The same is true as we run the race of the Christian life. The Perseverance of the Saints is a perseverance *with* the saints.

The writer of Hebrews shows us the ecosystem God designed for our persevering:

> "Watch out, brothers and sisters, so that there won't be in any of you an evil, unbelieving heart that turns away from the living God. But encourage each other daily, while it is still called 'today,' so that none of you is hardened by sin's deception. For we have become participants in Christ if we hold firmly until the end the reality that we had at the start."
>
> (Hebrews 3 v 12-14)

As we saw in the previous chapter on Irresistible Grace, God calls us to play a part in the way he saves his people. And God also calls us to play a part in the way he sustains his people. We watch out for one another's perseverance.

God's designed us to mutually encourage each other to endure "daily." Why daily? Because the flesh doesn't stop. Satan doesn't take weekends off or work part-time Monday through Friday. Neither can you—for the sake of your brothers and sisters. You need people who've got your back and are ready to bring you back when you wander. And you need to stand at the ready for others, for their struggles and their straying.

Humble Calvinism means being heavily invested in each others' eternal security. If you see something, say something. If you spot evidences of grace and growth in a brother or sister, encourage them. If you spot signs of unbelief, unrepentant actions, or ungodly attitudes, step up, not back. People need you to remind them of a blood-stained cross and an empty, echoing tomb, of the power of the Spirit today and the certainty of the return of the Son. You need people who will do the same for you.

We forget the communal nature of the Bible. Many of the New Testament letters were written in community and to a community. We can't persevere in the teachings of the Bible apart from the saints. Have you noticed how many "let us" verses there are in the New Testament? They call us to persevere with the saints. "Let us pursue what promotes peace and what builds up one another" (Romans 14 v 19), and "Let us cleanse ourselves from every impurity of the flesh and spirit, bringing holiness to completion in the fear of God" (2 Corinthians 7 v 1), and "Let us grow in every way into him who is the head—

Christ" (Ephesians 4 v 15). We read these verses and think, "I need to pursue, cleanse, grow," but we should read them and think, "*We* need to..." Christian community has bigger implications and motivations than a weekly Bible study with a sandwich platter. Later in Hebrews, we get a "let us" with a built-in horizon:

"Let us hold on to the confession of our hope without wavering, since he who promised is faithful. And let us watch out for one another to provoke love and good works, not neglecting to gather together, as some are in the habit of doing, but encouraging each other, and all the more as you see the day approaching." (Hebrews 10 v 23-25)

Hold fast to the gospel confession, and don't flake out on the fellowship of the saints on Sundays or during the week. You need it. Your church needs it. God wants you to see that Christian community is more than a means to simply get you through the week or a rough patch. While the community of the saints does that, it also does more. Hebrews says to encourage each other, more and more as you see Judgment Day approaching. You need Christian community so you can make it to the day Christ comes.

Taking Perseverance of the Saints seriously means making the effort, and bearing the cost, to be involved with the perseverance of other saints. Are you lukewarm toward other believers? Do you actually pray for others when you say you will? Do you pursue meeting up with those who are struggling, even though you know it'd be easier and more fun to meet with a Christian friend who's doing fine? Do you risk a comfortable friendship in order to give, with tears in your eyes, a necessary rebuke? Don't belittle the role of the saints in your perseverance, or your role in theirs.

We all lose our grip from time to time. But our Father's grip is greater than ours. If you are in Christ, you will always be in Christ. No sin can separate you from Christ. Jesus already paid for it. Humble Calvinism rests and rejoices in the hands of God. No anxious panic. No arrogant pride. No complacency, either. We persevere as saints, and with the saints. And we do so confidently and humbly, for from womb to tomb—from the Lamb's book of life to the marriage supper of the Lamb—we are in God's hands. And he never lets go.

8. HUMBLE AND HAPPY (AND CALVINIST)

I nerd out over the Hubble Space Telescope and the images it sends back to earth—the Cat's-Eye Nebula, Star Wars-ian images, and the heavens declaring the glory of God. So I'm excited about NASA's new awe-finder, the James Webb Telescope—except that it's grounded on earth. The $7.4-billion machine is in the shop because a few screws came loose, and the wrong kind of wiring messed up the voltage, and someone used the wrong solvent to clean the thrusters. Add up these three errors and you've got a launch date pushed back a few years—and $600 million more added to the bill. A beautiful machine, designed to discover beauty, now halted by human error.

Let's not let our human error keep Calvinism in the hangar. Let's tighten the screws. TULIP is meant to be a telescope of grace. It takes the bigness of God's redemptive work and shows it to us in pictures and points we can somewhat handle. Calvinism should leave us humbly thanking our Maker.

Humble Calvinism is no oxymoron. It's the real deal. Humility is what Calvinism was always meant to produce. When the points of TULIP get beyond our brains and embed in our hearts, then humility, thanksgiving, and graciousness grow on the branches of our speech, actions, and attitudes. Anything less is a misfire. A phony.

Abraham Kuyper, a turn-of-the-20th-century Calvinist pastor and author and (as if that wasn't enough) Prime Minister of the Netherlands, explains what makes a real Calvinist:

> "He only is the real Calvinist, and may raise the Calvinistic banner, who in his own soul, personally, has been struck by the Majesty of the Almighty, and yielding to the overpowering might of his eternal Love, has dared to proclaim this majestic love, over against Satan and the world, and the worldliness of his own heart, in the personal conviction of being chosen by God himself, and therefore of having to thank Him and Him alone, for every grace everlasting."[42]

Real Calvinism is a humble, God-enjoying, and loving-thy-neighbor Calvinism. Arrogance, lack of gentleness, impatience, and thinking we have the spiritual gift of street-fighting doesn't reveal a problem with the doctrines of grace but with our hearts.

---

42 Abraham Kuyper, *Lectures on Calvinism*, page 69.

GODLINESS IS THE GOAL

If we are fully "Calvinized" but godliness isn't growing, we need to reset the dials and check the wires from our heart to our head. Paul rebukes those who teach a doctrine that doesn't promote godliness:

> "If anyone teaches false doctrine and does not agree with the sound teaching of our Lord Jesus Christ and *with the teaching that promotes godliness*, he is conceited and understands nothing, but has an unhealthy interest in disputes and arguments over words. From these come envy, quarreling, slander, evil suspicions." (1 Timothy 6 v 3-4, my italics)

A properly planted TULIP *will* bloom into godliness. When we have a bloated zeal for arguments—a disproportionate desire to debate—we don't understand the grace we are trying to defend. Of course, there will be times to explain the doctrines of grace, and there will be times to defend them, but we should always be seasoned by grace, mercy, and love. The meek will inherit the earth—we will be okay if we don't prove our points.

John Newton reminds us Calvinists, "Of all people who engage in controversy, we, who are called Calvinists, are most expressly bound by our own principles to the exercise of gentleness and moderation."[43] Newton knew that the doctrines of grace should produce a profound graciousness.

---

43 John Newton and Richard Cecil, *The Works of John Newton*, Vol. 1, page 270.

A heart-grasp of Total Depravity means we are humbled by our sin, dependent on the power of the Spirit, and sympathetic toward every sinner and their struggles. Kindness flows from knowing our history.

A heart-knowledge of Unconditional Election leads us to the grandeur of God's grace, humbling us by the reality that God chose to save us based on nothing we are or have done. So, are we going to love and serve people only if they deserve it or give us something back? Not anymore.

Definite Atonement, when connected to head and heart, shows us the specific love Christ has for his church—local and global. It shows us how Jesus humbled himself to serve his people, empowering us to do the same for the student ministry in our church, the set-up and tear-down team, or the widow who needs her lawn mowed.

When the doctrine of Irresistible Grace breaks through our clogged hearts, we are humbled by the Spirit's relentless power to draw us to Christ, and we are honored to join our triune God in his mission to save sinners all around the world. Why would God invite you and me to do such a thing? Because he is merciful, gracious, and abounding in faithful love.

And once our heart is in rhythm with the pulse of the Perseverance of Saints, we are made both confident and humble, knowing that God keeps us from stumbling because without him, we wouldn't make it for a day—and we humbly help others keep going in faith.

Humble Calvinism—real Calvinism—is about both orthodoxy and orthopraxy: about right doctrine and the right practice, posture, and passion. Will you pursue it? Do any changes need to be made in your thinking? Living? Speech? Do some relationships need to be reconciled? Does forgiveness need to be sought? Begin today.

Calvinism is a pile of coal, mined from the depths of doctrine, that sets a fire blazing in our hearts that drives us down the track toward godliness. True Calvinism helps us love God with all our minds and hearts, and love our neighbors as ourselves. If your Calvinism doesn't do that, then check the coal; you might have a bad batch.

HAPPY EVER AFTER

Grouchy Christians are the worst. It's borderline blasphemy. "How joyful is the one whose transgression is forgiven, whose sin is covered!" (Psalm 32 v 1). Those whose hearts have been broadened by the doctrines of grace should no longer be cranky and cynical. No, we should be some of the largest-smiling, most-welcoming, joy-spreading people anyone could ever meet. "How happy is the one you choose and bring near to live in your courts!" (Psalm 65 v 4). Grace and gladness are always together. Spread the joy. Author Tony Reinke reminds us:

"When God breaks into our lives with the beauty of Jesus Christ, we find a true and solid and eternal joy. But of course, you and I know better than to say we found joy. Rather, joy found us—sometimes slowly, sometimes at warp speed. That is the story of TULIP. Calvinism is the story of a long-planned, sovereign joy that finds you before you even see it coming."[44]

Calvinism is the unfolding drama about a doctrine of joy forevermore. A story of living happily ever after.

Paul tells us to "Rejoice in the Lord always. I will say it again: Rejoice!" (Philippians 4 v 4). Holy happiness is the main export of Calvinism. Every point gives us reason to rejoice in the Lord. He loved us wretches before the foundation of the world. Praise God! No one's love is greater than God's—the Father sent his beloved Son, and the Son went to the cross for his friends. How can we not rejoice over the grace of Christ? God reeled us in when we were dead fish at the bottom of the lake, and he made us alive. (Are you smiling yet?) And God has taken it upon himself to make sure he doesn't lose any of his sheep. We are forever saved in Christ.

Whether you are finishing this book as a humbled Calvinist, or a still-being-humbled Calvinist, or a never-gonna-be-a Calvinist Christian, or an I-need-some-time-to-think-about-this-TULIP Christian, we can all affirm what Calvin says here: "Outside Christ there is nothing worth knowing."[45] Rejoice in the Lord always. Jesus over doctrine. Jesus because of doctrine. Jesus always. Christ is the center and cause of our knowing, living, rejoicing.

---

44 Tony Reinke, *The Joy Project: An Introduction to Calvinism*, page 124.

45 John Calvin, *Institutes of the Christian Religion* ed. John T. McNeill, trans. Ford Lewis Battles, Vol. 1, page 496.

Live with a holy happiness in God's sovereign and sustaining grace. Spread the word about the God who is rich in mercy, slow to anger, and abounding in faithful love. And for those of us who are happy to be called Calvinists, from now on let's make sure we are humble and happy Calvinists.

AFTERWORD
BY C.H. SPURGEON

Brothers, hold the five points of Calvinist doctrine, but don't hold them as babbling questions. What you have received of God, do not learn in order to fight with it, and to make contention and strife, and to divide the church of God, and rail against the people of the Most High, as some do. But, on the contrary, love one another as brothers and sisters, and hold the truth in love, and seek after the unity of the Spirit and the perfect bond of charity.

There are particular doctrinal brothers and sisters, good enough in their way, but still you can evidently see that the doctrine of election is a thing that they contend more for than the doctrine of the redemption of Christ; or if it be redemption, it is rather the speciality of redemption than the divine sacrifice itself. I love to preach the distinguishing grace of God, but I am far from thinking that some four or five points comprise all the truths which

God has revealed. Let us make it our aim to preach the doctrines with Christ as their sum and substance: as Dr. Robert Hawker preached them, "a full Christ for empty sinners." Let that be our theme. It is true to say that a ministry that seeks only to exalt doctrines has not the fullness of the Holy Spirit in it, for of the Holy Spirit it is written, "He shall glorify me" (John 16 v 14).

So do not give yourselves up to any system, and say, "I follow this doctor, or that." John Wesley is not our master—that is Jesus Christ. John Calvin is not our Master—that is Jesus Christ. These men were great and good: they were worthy of the love of all the church of God. But we do not call them Teacher. We may follow the man as far as the man follows Christ, but not an inch farther. We must sit at Jesus' feet: humble, teachable, and child-like.[46]

C.H. Spurgeon, Pastor,
Metropolitan Tabernacle, London

---

46 First Paragraph: "Who Is This?," in *The Metropolitan Tabernacle Pulpit Sermons*, Vol. 60, pages 95-96.
Second Paragraph: "The Holy Spirit Glorifying Christ," in *The Metropolitan Tabernacle Pulpit Sermons*, Vol. 8, page 460.
Third Paragraph: "Our Place; At Jesus' Feet," in *The Metropolitan Tabernacle Pulpit Sermons*, Vol. 35, pages 51-52.

BIBLIOGRAPHY

Michael F. Bird, *Evangelical Theology: A Biblical and Systematic Introduction* (Zondervan, 2013)

John Calvin, *Institutes of the Christian Religion* ed. John T. McNeill, trans. Ford Lewis Battles, Vol. 1 (Westminster John Knox Press, 2011)

John Calvin, *Sermon on Ephesians* (Banner of Truth, 1974)

John Calvin and James Anderson, *Commentary on the Book of Psalms*, Vol. 3 (Logos Bible Software, 2010)

John Calvin and William Pringle, *Commentary on the Book of the Prophet Isaiah*, Vol. 2 (Logos Bible Software, 2010)

John Calvin and William Pringle, *Commentaries on the Epistles of Paul to the Galatians and Ephesians* (Logos Bible Software, 2010)

John Calvin and William Pringle, *Commentaries on the Epistles to Timothy, Titus, and Philemon* (Logos Bible Software, 2010)

John Flavel, *The Complete Works of John Flavel*, Vol. 1 (Banner of Truth, 1968)

Ed. Jonathan and David Gibson, *From Heaven He Came and Sought Her: Definite Atonement in Historical, Biblical, Theological, and Pastoral Perspective* (Crossway, 2013)

Collin Hansen, *Young, Restless, and Reformed: A Journalist's Journey With the New Calvinists* (Crossway, 2008)

Joseph Haroutunian and Louise Pettibone Smith, *Calvin: Commentaries* (Westminster Press, 1958)

Marcus Peter Johnson, *One with Christ: An Evangelical Theology of Salvation* (Crossway, 2013)

Abraham Kuyper, *Lectures on Calvinism* (Eerdmans, 1931)

Martin Luther, *Commentary on Galatians* (Logos Research Systems, Inc., 1997)

Andrew Murray, *Humility* (B&H Books, 2017)

John Murray, *Redemption Accomplished and Applied* (Eerdmans, 1955)

John Newton and Richard Cecil, *The Works of John Newton* (Hamilton, Adams & Co., 1824)

J.I. Packer, *Evangelism and the Sovereignty of God* (IVP, 2012)

John Piper, God is the Gospel: Meditations on God's Love as the Gift of Himself (Crossway, 2005)

John Piper, *Five Points: Towards a Deeper Experience of God's Grace* (Christian Focus, 2013)

Michael Reeves, *Rejoicing in Christ* (IVP Academic, 2015)

Tony Reinke, *The Joy Project: An Introduction to Calvinism* (Desiring God/Cruciform Press, 2018)

Fleming Rutledge, *The Crucifixion: Understanding the Death of Jesus Christ* (Eerdmans, 2015)

Philip Schaff and David Schley Schaff, *History of the Christian Church*, Vol. 4 (Charles Scribner's Sons, 1910)

R.C. Sproul, *What is Reformed Theology? Understanding the Basics* (Baker, 2013)

C.H. Spurgeon, *The Metropolitan Tabernacle Pulpit Sermons* (Passmore & Alabaster, various)

C.H. Spurgeon, *The Sword and Trowel* (Passmore & Alabaster, 1874)

Jared C. Wilson, *Gospel Wakefulness* (Crossway, 2011)

ACKNOWLEDGMENTS

Books are barn-raisings. When raising a knotty beam or struggling to connect my thoughts, I could always count on my editor, Carl Laferton, to flex his editorial biceps. Whether sanding a splintery sentence or lopping off excess words, Carl made this book shine and stand in ways I couldn't have done on my own.

A big thanks to my agent, Don Gates, who took my proposed blueprints, believed in them, and found the right publisher to make *Humble Calvinism* a reality. Thanks to everyone at The Good Book Company who made sure this barn was a sturdy one.

Thank you, Ray Ortlund, not only for writing the foreword but for your ministry, kindness, and Jesus-fixation, which God used to change the course of my life, preaching, and affections.

Thanks to my kiddos, Ivy and Oliver. Your bedtime prayers for your Papa's book were answered by the Father in heaven. Natalie—my dear wife, the gem of Lake Charles—thank you for always encouraging me to write, to keep my tools sharp, and to keep going. Thanks for believing the barn would come together. Let's dance.

thegoodbook
COMPANY

BIBLICAL | RELEVANT | ACCESSIBLE

At The Good Book Company, we are dedicated to helping Christians and local churches grow. We believe that God's growth process always starts with hearing clearly what he has said to us through his timeless word—the Bible.

Ever since we opened our doors in 1991, we have been striving to produce Bible-based resources that bring glory to God. We have grown to become an international provider of user-friendly resources to the Christian community, with believers of all backgrounds and denominations using our books, Bible studies, devotionals, evangelistic resources, and DVD-based courses.

We want to equip ordinary Christians to live for Christ day by day, and churches to grow in their knowledge of God, their love for one another, and the effectiveness of their outreach.

Call us for a discussion of your needs or visit one of our local websites for more information on the resources and services we provide.

Your friends at The Good Book Company

thegoodbook.com | thegoodbook.co.uk
thegoodbook.com.au | thegoodbook.co.nz
thegoodbook.co.in